Susannah Martin
Convicted in Amesbury, Massachusetts, 1692, of "tempting men in their beds and appearing as a black hog with feet of bird." Object created in 1991: Raw wheat, silk, cord, guinea hen feet, steel bodice with Carrickmacross lace, steel nail; 42 x 8 x 6 inches.

Collection of Dr. P. Monroe Richmond, Virginia.

**Art by
Barbara Broughel**

Art Images

The cover design of this book is based on Barbara Broughel's work entitled "Martha Carrier". This powerful artistic expression is part of Broughel's series *Requiem*, which had been exhibited worldwide. The artist finds and researches the historical dissection between what we perceive American society to be and the reality that lies behind the perception. For *Requiem*, Broughel made an in-depth study of New England witchcraft trial cases, as well as the design of colonial American artifacts -- particularly household goods and clothing. Each of the objects in her *Requiem* series reflects a real trial and people, who were tried, convicted, or punished for witchcraft.

Art connoisseurs discovered the artistic beauty and historical value of her work very early in her career. A considerable number of the *Requiem* objects are in private collections today.

Front Cover:
Martha Carrier
Convicted in Andover, Massachusetts, 1692, of "carrying smallpox and bringing illness to neighbouring livestock." Object created in 1991: Chicken foot, lace bodice, and cotton bonnet; 6 x 3 x 2 inches.

Artist's Biography

Barbara Broughel is an artist based in New York City who teaches at the Massachusetts Institute of technology in Cambridge. She has had exhibitions at the Irish Museum of Modern Art, Dublin; the List Visual Arts Center, MIT, Cambridge; Kuntsmuseum des Kantons Thurgau, Warth, Switzerland; the Rothschild Gallery, Harvard University; Haines Art Gallery, Chapel Hill, North Carolina; and the San Jose Museum of Art, San Jose, CA. She is a recipient of numerous grants and awards for her work. Broughel holds a B.S. (1980) in Visual Arts from the University of California, San Diego, and a M.F.A. (1983) from the State University of New York, Buffalo.

To order more copies of this *AceN Press* book
or to learn more about the extraordinary art of
Barbara Broughel visit

www.witchrequiemgallery.com

AceN Press books are available also through

other Internet book stores.

AceN Press books are available at a special quantity discounts for bulk purchases intended for library purposes, sales promotions, premiums, fund raising or educational use.

AceN Press publishes books on the relationship between science and the occult. We encourage new authors to submit their manuscripts for consideration.

AceN Press,
138 West Dana Street, Suite C,
Mountain View, CA 94041, USA

HOW DO WITCHES FLY?

A Practical Approach to Nocturnal Flights

By Alexander Kuklin

AceN Press
Mountain View, CA, U.S.A.

HOW DO WITCHES FLY?
A Practical Approach to Nocturnal Flights
by Alexander Kuklin

Published by:
 AceN Press
 Mountain View, CA, USA

All rights reserved. Reproduction or translation of any part of this book beyond that permitted by Section 107 or 108 of the 1976 United States Copyright Act without the permission of the copyright owner is unlawful. Requests for permission or further information should be addressed to the Publisher.

Copyright 1999 by Alexander Kuklin
First printing 1999
Printed in the United States of America

Library of Congress Catalog Card Number: 98-96113

Library of Congress Cataloging-in-Publishing Data
Kuklin, Alexander

How do witches fly?: A Practical Approach to Nocturnal Flights / by Alexander Kuklin - 1st Ed.

    p. cm.
    Includes bibliographical references and index.
    ISBN 0-9664027-0-7

    1. Witches – Rituals – Ointment. 2. Herbs. I. Title
    2. New Age – Plants
    3. Biochemistry - Alkaloids

Direct all inquiries to *AceN Press,* 138 West Dana Street, Suite C, Mountain View, CA 94041, USA

98-96113
CIP

Warning - Disclaimer

To the reader

CAUTION

The plants and animals discussed in preparation of the witches' ointment are **highly poisonous**. Any experimentation with them is strongly discouraged. The author and the publisher do not assume any responsibility for incorrect use of and experiments with the plants discussed in this book.

Vos igitur, doctrinae et sapientiae filii, perquirite in hoc libro colligendo nostram dispersam intentionem quam in diversis locis proposuimus et quod occultatum ets a nobis in uno loco, manifestatum fecimus illud in alio, ut sapientibus vobis patefiat.

Henricus Cornelius Agrippa ab Nettesheym
De Occulta Philosophia
Liber Tertius, Cap. LXV

Only for you, children of doctrine and knowledge, have we written this work. Examine this book, ponder the meaning we have dispersed in various parts and gathered again; what we have concealed in one place we have disclosed in another, that it may be understood by your wisdom.

Henrich Cornelius Agrippa von Nettesheim
De Occulta Philosophia, 3,65

PREFACE

Voluminous literature exists on European witchcraft and historical analyses on the subject are sometimes contradictory. This book discusses only one aspect of the diabolical practice, namely the preparation of the "flying" ointment. The existence of this mysterious ointment and its use during witchcraft ceremonies has been an important issue of Inquisitorial trials. However, exact recipes for its preparation are lost.

The author has tried to pharmacologically dissect the witches' preparation. The use of the ointment as a hallucinogen before witches' gatherings is discussed in terms of available scientific data and field experiences.

The author is indebted to the researchers who have accumulated knowledge and analyzed witchcraft in various aspects. Their contributions have been listed in the Bibliography at the end of the book. An attempt to cite all the authorities and sources consulted in the preparation of this book has not been made due to space limitations.

Acknowledgements are extended to the Balkan herbalists whose knowledge and friendship has been a major source for this book. I thank Peter O'Rourke for his editorial comments.

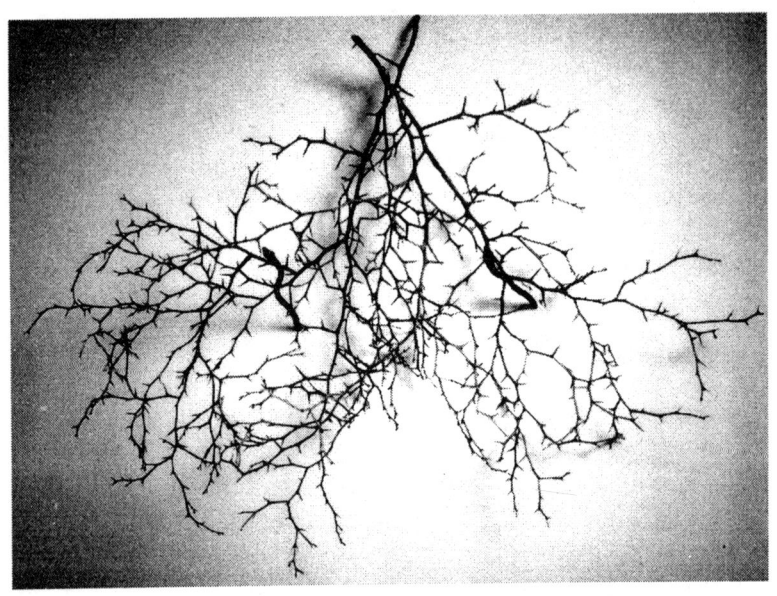

Nathaniel and Rebecca Greensmith

Convicted in Hartford, Connecticut, 1662, of "intending to make merry on Christmas" and "fornicating with the Devil," respectfully.
Object created in 1991; Wrought steel and wild orange briar; 36 x 42 x16 inches.

Art by Barbara Broughel

TABLE OF CONTENTS

Introduction...................................	1
One	
The Flying Ointment...........................	3
Two	
Metamorphosis.................................	13
Three	
Ointment Ingredients..........................	17
Four	
Toxins in Plants and Animals..................	25
Five	
Animal Ingredients............................	33
Six	
Herbs used in the Flying Ointment.............	41
Seven	
Ointment Preparation..........................	75
Eight	
Mechanisms of the Ointment Action.............	81
Nine	
Flying on a Broom.............................	93
Ten	
Nocturnal Flights.............................	97

Glossary.. 99

Appendix... 101

Bibliography.. 103

Index to scientific and common names....... 109

INTRODUCTION

> "It is astonishing that there should still be people who do not believe in witches. For my part I suspect that the truth is that such people really believe in their hearts, but will not admit it ..."
>
> Henry Boquet, *An Examen of Witches* (1602 A.D.)

T he Sabbat appeared as a term in witch trial records in the Carcasonne and Toulouse regions in France shortly after 1340 A.D. according to historical studies. The Sabbat stands for the assembly of the witches on certain days of the year. Numerous people who belonged to the infernal cult attended these gatherings; they worshipped the Devil. Even earlier (circa 1006 A.D.), some women claimed that on certain nights they accompanied an army of demons and went to the gathering place in the silence of the night, leaving their sleeping husbands at home.

- How did witches fly?
- Was the broom their true vehicle?

Historical records show that witches prepared themselves for their meeting by cooking a magic ointment. They rubbed their bodies with this mysterious ointment before flying to the Sabbat. During the trial of the Summerset witches in England in 1664 A.D. the accused Elisabeth Style said that "before they [the witches] are carried to their meetings, they anoint their foreheads, and hand-wrists with an Oyl the Spirit brings them (which smells raw) and then they are carried in a very short time, using these words as they pass *Thout, tout a tout, tout, throughout and about."* Her accomplice Alice Duke supported this statement by adding that the oil was greenish in color.

- What was that ointment?
- Did witches really fly?
- Why did they use the ointment?
- What ingredients did witches include in this preparation?
- How did their concoctions work?

These are the questions that this book attempts to address. The lore of using certain plants for preparing the witches' ointment has not been lost. The secrets of the ointment are revealed in this book. The intricacies of its preparation are discussed and the mechanisms of the ointment action explained.

I speculate that the witches' ointment was the biggest jewel in the crown of Medieval pharmacology. This herbal concoction was a poison to the layman but a spiritual tool to the Believer of the craft. Its psychedelic effects were powerful and unexplainable at the time. Here I try to analyze the available data about the ointment ingredients and give an explanation for the ointment action based on analysis of its chemical composition.

Experimentation with any recipes for preparation of the ointment is not recommended. Scientific explanations of the ointment do not make it accessible to everybody. The practice of anointing with this herbal preparation is still an esoteric field.

Chapter 1

THE FLYING OINTMENT

> *"You know 'tis precious to transfer*
> *Our 'nointed flesh into the air,*
> *In moonlight nights."*
>
> Middleton, *The Witch*

In the fourteenth century, Lady Alice Kyteler in Ireland was arrested and tried for heresy and sorcery. She claimed that during diabolical rituals she and her accomplices summoned the demon Robin Artisson, who appeared in shapes of either an animal or a man. This statement was confirmed by the confessions of an accomplice, Petronilla of Meath, who was burned as a consequence of her complicity. Lady Alice Kyteler also confessed that during one of the meetings the demon taught her how to prepare ointments of loathsome composition.

In many other Inquisition trials the accused witches confessed that they acquired knowledge of how to prepare a certain ointment during their meeting with the Devil who appeared in various forms. The Devil assumed the forms of a demon or man but most often that of a he-goat. The witches' Master revealed the secrets of the ointment which served as a link between him and the witches, and as a means for the witches to prepare for the journey to the Sabbat.

By definition, an ointment is a preparation in which a drug is suspended or dissolved in grease or oil. Compelling evidence from trial records shows that witches cooked herbs in oil and anointed themselves before the Sabbat meeting.

The mysterious ointment existed but the art for its preparation has remained oblivious. Details about its ingredients and preparation are vague but not insufficient and they are the subject of my investigation.

Information about the ointment comes from the records of Anne-Marie de Georgel's trial from Toulouse in the fourteenth century. The accused confessed to being taken to the Sabbat by a he-goat who explained poisonous plants to her. She admitted that she had boiled poisonous herbs and substances taken from the bodies of animals or humans in a cauldron.

The accounts of an ointment used before going to the Sabbat, extracted from the Inquisition victims, are supported by the comments of the inquisitors themselves. A theorist for the persecutions in the Swiss part of Europe was the theologian Johannes Nider. Between 1435 and 1437 A.D. he wrote a book, which goes by the name of *Formicarius*. In this book Nider described that witches cooked beans and cock's testicles in cauldrons from which ointments were made. The remaining liquid from this process was stored in bottles and given to new initiates to drink. Pascual de Andagoya (1495-1548 A.D.), a conquistador exploring the Darien region in Spain, claimed to have found witches and sorcerers among the native population who anointed themselves with oils supposedly given to them by the Devil.

Evidence of the ointment appeared consistently in the trial records all over Europe. Why did the Devil teach his followers to prepare the mysterious ointment? What was its purpose?

An answer to this question is found in the writings of the Mediaeval researcher Martin Delrio. He explained the use of the ointment as follows: "The Devil is able to convey them [the witches] to the Sabbat without the use of any unguent, and often he does so. But for several reasons he prefers that they should anoint themselves. Sometimes when the witches seem afraid it serves to encourage them. When they are young and tender they will be thus better able to bear the hateful embrace of the Satan who has assumed the shape of a man. For by this horrid anointing he dulls their senses and persuades these deluded wretches that there is some great virtue in the viscid lubricant."

The above comment is supported also by the opinion of Henry Bouquet, who was the High Justice of the district of Saint-Clad in France. He is considered to be one of the chief authorities on the subject. Bouquet died in 1616 A.D. but the first edition of his book *Discourse Des Sorceress* appeared 14 years before his death. In his book he wrote "...Sometimes they [witches] anoint themselves with ointment, & sometimes not... There are some people, who although they are not Sorcerers, if they are anointed, are none the less carried off Sabbat."

A similar opinion comes from a representative of the authorities in Italy. Arnaldo Albertini was the inquisitor of Sicily and Bishop of Patti who died in 1544 A.D. He wrote a book designed to guide inquisitors during trials and is frequently referred to by subsequent writers. The book was published in 1553 A.D. by his successor in Palermo. In his book he wrote about an ointment prepared by witches by which means they were transported to the places of their meetings.

It was a popular belief that witches flew to their gathering place during the night. Thus, in the seventeenth century witches in Germany were reported to anoint themselves with the fat of cats or wolves, asses' milk and to fly out of their houses riding broom sticks.

The belief in the flight to the Sabbat on certain nights was questioned by early Mediaeval researchers. The famous Benedictine Abbot Regino of Prume (906 A.D.) wrote in his book *De ecclesiasticis disciplinis* that the excursion through the air was generally preceded by an unction with a magic ointment. However, he stated "..certain utterly abandoned women, turning aside to follow Satan, being seduced by the illusions and phantasmical shows of demons firmly believe and openly profess that in the dead of night they ride upon certain beasts along with the pagan goddess Diana." According to Abbot Regino the witches "believed" that they flew and in reality the flight did not occur. This will be discussed in detail later in the book.

The ointment was applied to various parts of the body. Trial records show repeatedly that the witches talked about anointing not only their body but also their brooms.* Thus, during the trial of five women charged with witchcraft at Arras in 1460 A.D., the following confession was recorded: "When they desired to go to the said sorcery, with an ointment which the Devil had delivered to them they anointed a wooden rod which was but small and their palms and their wholehand likewise; and so, putting this small rod between their legs, straightway they flew there where they wished to be, above good towns and woods and waters, and the Devil guided them to that place where they must hold their assembly."

An anonymous text written after 1626 A.D. and included in a book published in Halle (Germany), in 1703 A.D. discusses the flying to the Sabbat on brooms, forks, sticks, etc. According to the author witches prepared the ointment from somniferous herbs as the Devil instructed them. They smeared themselves and their brooms or forks and fell into deep sleep, dreaming that they were flying. An explanation of this ritual is provided in following chapters.

The ointment was used for flying not only to the Sabbat. Peter Binsfeld, in his book *Tractatus de*

---

* For discussions on the role of the broom see Chapter Nine.

Confessionibus Maleficorum described a case in which a young woman from Bergamo was found naked in the bed of her young cousin in Venice, Italy. She said that the night before she had seen her mother get up during the night, strip and anoint herself with an unguent from a pot which she took from a hiding place and then she disappeared. The girl was extremely curious and followed her example. She found herself in the chamber of the young boy of Venice and to her surprise, her mother was there too. Both were terrified but the girl invoked the name of Christ and the Virgin. The mother disappeared and the daughter remained.

According to several records the flying ointment was used also to prevent husbands from recognizing the absence of their wives during the night when they went to the Sabbat. Peter Osterman, a law professor at the University of Cologne and president of public disputations published a literary work in 1629 A.D., in which he described such cases. One woman put her husband into profound sleep by touching his ear with the ointment used for flying. Another woman put a bundle of straw in the bed where she was supposed to be lying by her husband and used the ointment on him. But then why did not these men fly to the Sabbat and stayed in their beds? It is probable that the ointment was of different composition or used in a small dosage as it could be seen later in the this book.

A question, which bothered Mediaeval and contemporary researchers on the subject, is whether claims about the witches' ointment were true. Numerous jurisdiction books and clerical manuals for the inquisitors were published during the Middle Ages. They gave instructions to the persecutors as to what proofs they should look for in order to find a witch. According to Franciscus Bordonus, the consultor to the Inquisitor in Rome, one of the indica (indicum is singular) to prove diabolical sorcery sufficient for torture is "... The assertion of one who has seen the accused anoint or give drink to a man or animal and they have soon sickened or died." Another indicum, which established a commitment of crime was the finding of " a pot full of human limbs, scary things, images, hosts, etc..."

It was a practice of the Inquisition of Spain as according to a Madrid Instruction, never to arrest unless they find a definite proof. Among the things listed as such proofs were unguents used by witches.

Despite the huge number of witch trials and meticulous documentation of the confessions, facts concerning the ointments are contradictory. For example, one of the three judges who took part in the trials in Spain in 1610 A.D. was the inquisitor Alonso de Salazar y Frias. He and his assistants were able to find twenty-two cauldrons and a list of ointments, powders and other concoctions. Although material evidence was found in this case, Alonso de Salazar stated in his reports that experiments performed under the supervision of doctors proved the absurdity of these ointments. He reached the conclusion that the majority of acts attributed to witches never occurred.

Another case in which the ointment was found in evidence during a trial was reported by the Spanish doctor Laguna. He was in service of the Duke of Lorraine around 1545 A.D. During this time his master became seriously ill, an elderly couple was suspect. The poor people confessed under torture to the practice of witchcraft and of causing the Duke's illness. Their death-sentence was stayed because they claimed they could cure the Duke. Indeed, the Duke of Lorraine recovered soon after their intervention. The authorities found a green-colored, bad smelling ointment in the house of the arrested witches. Laguna wrote that "the odor of this unguent was so heavy and oppressive that it seemed to be composed of the very coldest and soporific herbs: which are the cicuta, the night-shade, the henbane and the mandragore." The doctor became interested in the ointment and decided to perform an experiment. He rubbed the ointment all over the body of a volunteer who happened to be the wife of the city-executioner. This lady suffered a loss of sleep, anxiety and became extremely jealous of her husband (obvious symptoms of neurosis). As soon as she was anointed, she fell into a deep stupor. It took Dr. Laguna much effort to wake her up after thirty-six hours. The lady told him of her extraordinary dreams during the time she was under the influence of this narcotic. Dr. Laguna had studied Dioscorides (circa 60 A.D. in Greece) whose writings had been considered an authority on medicinal substances for over 1,500 years. The doctor knew about a plant causing unbelievable visions in people during their sleep. Laguna concluded that the ointment contained the extracts of that or a similar plant.

A similar experiment aiming to establish the power of the witches' preparations was performed by the scientists Gassendi and Malebranche in the sixteenth century. Gassendi gave a narcotic to several people in a Basses Alps village. The potion had been prepared from a recipe obtained by Gassendi from a sorcerer. The villagers fell into a deep sleep after which they told strange happenings.

A "pipe of ointment" was found in the house of Dame Alice Kyteler of Kilkenny who was arrested in 1324 A.D. upon the accusation of going to the Sabbat as discussed previously. She confessed that she greased a staff with the ointment "upon which she ambolled and galloped through thick and thin."

In contrast to the above cases, the judge De Lancre claimed in his writings that they were never able to find the slightest trace of ointments for examination purposes. Like other authors, he wrote about ointments, mentioned by the victims during interrogations, but did not give any particular details about their composition. The lack of evidence was also recorded in the case of the witch Maria de Illarra, whose trial took place in Fuenterrabia in 1611 A.D. Two town councilors interrogated many witnesses. Among them was a thirteen year old girl who made the statement that Maria de Illarra had anointed her under the arms. Then she seized the girl by the shoulders and flew with her out of the house. Maria de Illarra admitted being a witch on May 6th, 1611 A.D. She told the judges how she had been initiated in witchcraft and among other things she mentioned the ointment the witches used to rub on their chests (down as far as the naval) and under their armpits before flying through the air. The interrogators wanted to know where she kept the pot with the ointment. She said she had thrown it away a week before and that it had broken in pieces. Nothing incriminating was found among her belongings.

The belief in the existence of the flying ointment was documented in prints from the Middle Ages. In his *Pictorial Anthology of Witchcraft, Magic & Alchemy*, de Givry reproduced three prints of Hans Baldung dated 1514 A.D. One of the prints shows four witches engaged in the preparation of the unguent or as he called it, "the sorcerer's grease." One witch is grinding drugs in a little cauldron and "the others are looking, with admiration and envy, at an old witch, more diligent than themselves, who is already riding among the clouds on her way to the Sabbath, mounted on her fork, and followed by a goat." Another print portrays the witches anointing their fork with the already prepared unguent. The last print depicts a witch seated backward upon a goat. She carries a cauldron between the prongs of her fork. A second cauldron can be seen boiling above a fire of vervain, and a third pours out steam charged with malefic elements.

An assembly of witches preparing the ointment is depicted in a wood-engraving in the old German book *Die*

Emeis by Dr. Johanes Geiler published by the house of Gruninger at Strasburg in 1517 A.D. As in Baldung's prints, the witches are shown naked.

In a print by Jaspar Isaak from the sixteenth century, *Abomination des Sorciers* one can see almost all the elements of the Satanic art used in the process of preparation for the Sabbat. The wall cupboard shelves on the left side of

Witches' Sabbat, Frans Franken II, a courtesy of the Graphische Sammlung Albertiena, Vienna, Austria (Inv. No. 7971).

the print contain pots and flasks probably holding unguents and drugs. A sieve perhaps used in divination is also seen. There is more glassware depicted on the print than seen in a chemist's laboratory shown in "The Chymist" by David Teniers the Younger (the 17th century).

The picture "An assembly of witches" by Frans Francken (1581-1642 A.D.) exhibited in the

Kunsthistorisches Museum at Vienna depicts an old woman rubbing the unguent on the back of a naked witch. Two other witches are stirring the contents of the cauldron and blowing the fire, and a third is reading a Black book. Similar scenes are found in a painting of Teniers, now lost but preserved as a print by the engraver Aliamet.

Objects of witchcraft in England have been collected in the Pitt Rivers Museum, Oxford. Among them is a small glass flask of bilobed shape, silvered over the inside and stoppered. The flask has been reputed to contain a witch. An old lady living in a village near Hove gave the bottle to the museum in 1915, remarking "They do say there be a witch in it, and if you let un out there'll be a peck o'trouble." Probably such flasks were used to store love philtres or poisons.

A majority of the Pitt Rivers exhibits were used in sympathetic magic. In this practice the witch casts a spell or manipulates an object that has been in contact with or resembles a person. This ritual causes the desired detrimental effect on the chosen victim. Some plants used in sympathetic magic have also been obtained by the museum. An onion stuck with pins and accompanied by a paper with a name on it was donated by Lady Taylor's ancestors after her death in 1921. A lemon studded with nails was found hidden at the top of some furniture in the house of an English grocer in Naples. The lemon was used as witchcraft against him. It was presented to the museum by his granddaughter Mrs. Veronic Berry in 1967.

In contrast to sympathetic magic, the flying magic depended on the ingredients used in the potion. The ratio of the various herbs used in the ointment was the key to unlocking its power.

Chapter 2

METAMORPHOSIS

> "...she [Pamphile the witch]...rubbed her body therewith from the sole of the foot to the crown of the head: and when she had spoken much privily with the lamp, and shaked all the parts of her body, and as they gently moved, behold I perceive a plume of feathers did burgeon out upon them, strong wings did grow, her nose was more crooked and hard, her nails turned into claws, and so Pamphile became an owl..."
>
> Apuleius, *The Golden Ass*

A record from the fifteenth century describes the involvement in witchcraft of a young man, Pierre, who swore allegiance to the Devil for money. Pierre was given an ointment by a certain Michael Verdung and he rubbed his body with it. The young man was struck by terror when he noticed that he was turning into a wolf. His companion joined him in this experience. Both were restored to their human forms after they were anointed by familiar demons.

The mysterious witches' ointment has been described in stories according to which the witches transformed into animals, predominantly wolves. The transformation into a wolf is termed *lycanthropy*. The wolf has been feared through the centuries because of its power to kill, its ability to hunt in packs and insatiable taste for blood. The wolf kills as many sheep in the herd as he can, yet takes only one. Man's hatred for this animal has driven it to near extinction.

A well known French story from the sixteenth century tells us of a hunter who was attacked by a wolf. The hunter managed to pull out his knife and cut one of the animal's paws off. He put the paw in his hunting bag and went home. On the way he met a friend and told him the story. He reached in his bag to show his friend the paw but instead of a paw he was shocked to find a woman's hand with a golden ring on one of the fingers. The hunter was terrified to recognize the ring and the hand as his wife's. He rushed home and found his wife whose bandaged arm was soaked in blood. The woman was tried as a witch and burned at the stake.

Werewolves were also known in the Eastern parts of the European continent. During the Mediaeval period these lands were under the Turkish yoke. The Ottoman Turks (named after Osman, the first ruler of their dynasty) set foot on the Balkan peninsula in the middle of the fourteenth century. In 1453 A.D. the Turks seized Constantinople and made it their capital. Their power grew and they conquered not only the Bulgarians but Greeks, Albanians, Serbs, Armenians and Arabs. This is the period when Europe's population decreased after the plague which raged through the continent. The Turkish armies were only stopped at the gates of Vienna. Christianity was suppressed on the Balkan Peninsula. The idea about witches in this part of Europe was different from the West.

Many magic pagan rituals are preserved in the Balkan countries until today and some of them are commented on later. These ancient beliefs mixed with Christian religion are of importance for the analysis of witchcraft in Western Europe and later in the United States.

In contrast to the transformation of witches into

werewolves are the "werewolf demons" who were believed to originate from the souls of the unbaptized dead and the victims of murders. In Bulgaria, these demons, named *karakondzhuli*, appear between Christmas and Epiphany in animal forms (as wolves, mad dogs, and horses) or deformed men. The time of their appearance is called the "dog days" or "unbaptized days." They break into houses and vandalize everything valuable. Helpless victims caught outside during the "dog days" are ridden on by them. People's fear of these winter demons was enormous and stories are still told by very old people in the mountainous regions of the Balkan called also Stara Planina. A transition from werewolf demons representing the world of the dead, to the witches who transform into werewolves is found in Romania, where the werewolves were called *prikulici* and *virolac*, and in Slovene bearing the name *vedomec*. These were either demons or human beings able to transform into a wolf.

Transformations into animals have been described in the Latin literature. Thus, in *The Golden Ass* of Apuleius, the witch Pamphile decided to transform herself into a bird. The hero of Apuleius' story, Lucius looked through a crack in the door and saw the witch Pamphile disrobed and took out of a coffer many different kinds of boxes. She opened one of them and anointed her entire body with the ointment from Lucius saw with amazement that the witch grew wings, a beak, and claws, and thus transformed into an owl.

The transformation of witches into animals has a long history related to peoples' beliefs and traditions. The use of the flying ointment in European witchcraft in such metamorphosis contributed further to these beliefs via the effects of the ointment ingredients on the mind of the practitioners. Experimental data support this hypothesis and are discussed in the following chapters.

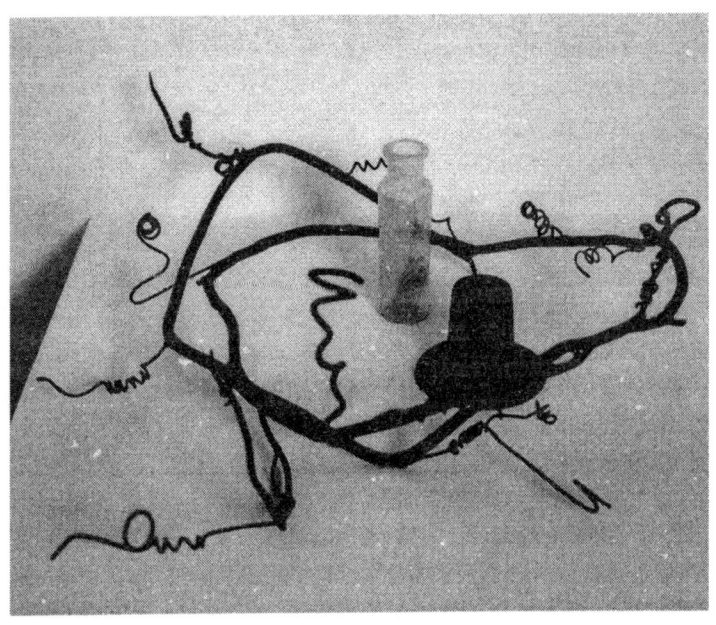

Martha and Giles Cory
Convicted in Salem Farms, Massachusetts, 1692, of having his apparition attend merry meetings" and "manufacturing witch pins and mysterious ointments," respectfully.
Object created in 1991: Wrought steel "grapevine" crown, brass hat, glass bottle with steel pins; 46 x 10 x 10 inches.
Art by Barbara Broughel

Chapter 3

OINTMENT INGREDIENTS

> *"Round about the cauldron go;*
> *In the poison'd entrails throw,-"*
>
> Shakespeare, *Macbeth*

Mediaeval artists and authors have always been fascinated by the witches' cauldron. Many prints and paintings from the Middle Ages depict busy witches in preparation of their magic ointment which will take them to the Sabbat. But what did they put in the cauldron? What did they cook?

Shakespeare in his play *Macbeth* alludes to the use of a mysterious broth cooked by the witches. Middleton as well elaborates on a preparation in his play entitled *The Witch*.

- Were these writers creating fiction or were they pointing out a dramatic truth?
- What were the real ingredients for the witches' brew and unguent?
- What was magic about them?

The original recipes of the witches' ointment have not been discovered. Practicing witches or herbalists accused in witchcraft during the Middle Ages were in most cases illiterate. Herbal recipes were passed orally from one generation to another. The inquisitors kept good records during trials but details of the preparation of the flying ointment are difficult to find. However, books of physicians who were present during some of the trials or researchers of Nature during the Mediaeval period are valuable sources in regard to the ointment preparation. Some sorcerers or magicians also made notes of what they learned about the ointment. From these sources we learn about the witches' pharmacopoeia. It consisted of substances from the animal and plant kingdoms and they will be analyzed in detail in the following chapters.

R_x

animal ingredients:
    fat, toad, salamander
plant ingredients:
    radix, folia or *herba Atropae beladonnae*
    folia Hyosciami nigri
    folia Daturae stramonii
    folia Digitalis purpuraea

and other plants

Prepare *legae artis*

One of the books that often cited in literary discussions on witchcraft throughout the centuries is the aforementioned *De prestigiis daemonum*. Its author, Johann Weyer had knowledge of old medical books discussing plant properties. He was also well acquainted with theological texts dealing with witchcraft and Inquisitorial records. Dr.

Weyer explicitly discussed the methods used by the "evildoers", i.e. the practitioners of witchcraft. Among the employed methods Weyer described that "plants, animals, and parts of animals - whether for superstitious reasons or by way of deceit" were used. Dr. Weyer clearly stated that he did not "wish to enumerate here those monstrous things which God will one day wish to destroy utterly." However, he meticulously listed the "monstrous" ingredients and this list represents an interesting but not always useful source to understand what plants were used by the witches. He listed, "Coracesia, Callicia, Menais, Corinthas, and Aproxis - herbs made famous by Pythagoras, with names certainly apt to terrify by their sound (and perhaps invented for that reason), and along with the Chirocineta of Democritus, and Agloaphotis, Marmaritis, Achemenis (Pliny relates that when this herb is thrown into the battle-line of the enemy the ranks become alarmed and turn to flee), Hippophanas, Adamantis, the Cynocephalaea of Apion, and other such terrifying and monstrous plants used by magicians but now banished from memory and totally abolished, by the singular goodness of God and the benefit of mankind."

It is clear that Weyer is talking about plants that were known to the physicians of ancient Greece. Some of the names unfortunately, have presented difficulties to the researchers in the identification of the corresponding plants. Discussions on the use of the individual plants could be found further in this book.

In the chapter of Weyer's book dedicated to the ointments used by witches he wrote that "*Lamiae* (instructed by their deceitful master) anoint themselves, rubbing the preparation into the skin. Then they believe that they will soon fly up the chimney and roam far and wide..." The author of *De prestigiis daemonum* was convinced that the ointment existed but his comment that the witches "believed" that they were flying describes well his explanation of the ointment effects.

Johann Weyer based his comments on a very respected source of the occult science during his time, i.e. the writings of the "most adroit investigator of the occult", Giovanni Battista Porta of Naples. Porta (156 A.D.) had this to say about the ointment, "I shall report what I have been told by these women. Cooling down the fat of children in a brazen vessel, they take it from the water, and thicken the final residue from the boiling. Then they store it and make constant use of it. They mix in wild celery, aconite, poplar leaves, and soot. In another method of preparation, they work together water parsnip, common acorum, cinque-foil, bat's blood, sleep inducing nightshade, and oil (they may mix in other ingredients, but they will be comparable)...." From this recipe we get a clearer idea how the mysterious witches' unguent was prepared.

Weyer proceeded further in his explanations by reporting the recipes of another respected writer of his time Girolamo Cardano. The unguent consisted of the "fat of young children, the juices of parsley, aconite, cinque-foil, and nightshade, and some soot." According to the same source, *Lamiae* fed upon parsley, chestnuts, beans, onions, cabbages, and phasels, all of which provoke turbulent dreams.

A recipe given by Cardano on the preparation of a sleep producing oil and quoted in *De prestigiis daemonum* is as follows: "Take seeds of darnel, henbane, hemlock, red and black poppy, lettuce, and purslain- four parts each- and one part of the berries of the soporific nightshade. From all these ingredients, let an oil be made up in accordance with the rules of the art, and for each once of this oil let one scruple of Theban opium be mixed in. Let one scruple of the mixture be taken, or one and one-half scruples, and a two day sleep will result."

Cardano wrote also about a liquid "producing sleep in wondrous fashion" but he did not wish to make the recipe public. He continued further with "darnel, *faba inversa*, opium, henbane, hemlock, different species of poppy, soporific nightshade *furiosum*, mandrake, water lily, and other herbs, by all of which one intelligence is either taken away or confused, so that the user seems demented in speaking, hearing, and responding, or falls into a very deep sleep for several days. But I have preferred to wrap their use in silence, and also the manner of making from them waters, wines, powders, lozenges, oils, and other preparations, lest I seem to have furnished someone the opportunity to abuse them. The most beneficent Author of all good has bestowed upon me the desire always to help and never to harm."

Cardano's position on the secrecy of the ointment preparation makes it clear why the recipe was obliterated by the ages. He, like many other authors and medical doctors did not wish to write about the ointment because of either guilty consciences or professional ethics. The ointment was a means for Satan to stay in contact with his followers and explicit comments on the unguent's preparation in religious texts endangered the writers. Physicians did not wish to discuss the ointment because it contained extremely dangerous poisons as will be seen from further discussions.

Another trustworthy source for the flying ointment recipes is Andres a Laguna, known as Lacuna in the Latin literature who was mentioned earlier. He was born in Segovia, Spain in 1499 A.D. and studied medicine in Paris (starting 1534 A.D.). Laguna returned to Spain and in 1539 A.D. earned the degree of Doctor of Medicine in Toledo. The same year he became a court physician and accompanied the Spanish King in his campaign to Flanders.

Laguna was also a prolific writer and deeply involved in public and religious affairs. His views on witchcraft could be found in a book about Dioscorides published in 1566 A.D.: "Dioscorides says that if a dram of the root of nightshade (carrier of madness) is drunk with wine there will be produced certain vain fantasmagorias which are at the same time very agreeable: it is to be understood that these visions are produced during sleep. That must be too (as I believe) the virtue of some unguents with which it was customary to anoint witches..." To confirm this, he tells the story about the old couple who bewitched the Duke Francis of Lorraine mentioned already in the section of the harmful ointments. He pointed out that "a pot half full of certain green unguent like white poplar ointment was found in the housed of the accused. The odor was very heavy and the physician recognized the smell of the "cicuta, night-shade, the henbane and the mandragore."

All the above sources are from physicians who had contact with reach and poor people. These medical doctors had some botanical knowledge and access to written and spoken information concerning witch trials. Their recipes are more trustworthy than what is found sometimes in sorcerers' books.

Mediaeval sorcerers used mainly two books as manuals for summoning spirits of different nature. These books were *Le Clavicule de Salomon* (The Book of Solomon) and *Le Grimoire du Pape Honorius*. They were accessible mostly to the educated people, physicians and learned sorcerers. Tradition required that a true sorcerer should posses the book(s) in manuscript, written by his own hand if possible. Therefore, the owners were either educated or people of means who could pay somebody to copy the book.

The book of Solomon, whose wisdom is praised in the Bible, is of great interest to the student of Nature. Hereon, Solomon commented on every tree and little flower, beasts, birds, reptiles, and fish. This knowledge of natural sciences was accompanied by theological and philosophical thought. His book, sometimes referred to as the Black book, passed from the Byzantine to the Latin speaking sorcerers in the thirteenth century. It should be noted that the learned men of the past who studied the secrets of Nature were labeled sorcerers. The Latin version of the book is attributed to Pope Honorius III who was suspected of sorcery. The books and manuscripts were devoted mainly to procedures of demon evocations. Rarely, they mention a plant used in the procedures and it is noteworthy that the sorcerers' plants were these found in the witches' pharmacopoeia.

Recipes connected to witchcraft of different nature are found in older than the Middle Ages literary sources. For example, Apulleius mentions in his *The Golden Ass* an "antidote" for the witches' ointment. When Pamphile had to assume the human shape, her maid gave her a bath and a drink, both composed of a bit of anise and some laurel leaves mixed with spring water.

From the above descriptions and records of witch trials it becomes clear that several plants and a few animals were used for the preparation of the ointment. Some of the plants are very dangerous poisons and are barely mentioned in contemporary herbal books. Others are used in preparations for curing various diseases and were well known to ancient and Mediaeval herbalists. Witches had their choices from the long list of plants. Among these plants, two or three are the major effective components of the mysterious unguent. The mastery in the preparation is choosing the right plants in a very specific proportion which will be discussed later in the book.

Previously discussed were the precautions taken by authorities against the use of pain killing potions by witches. Pain killers have been used since ancient times. Weyer tells the story of four monks of the Order of Preachers at Berne who in the year 1509 A.D. "maddened the mind of a lay brother and dulled his senses, as it were, by means of some such poisonous potion, that he was able to endure caustic or burning water [acid] without feeling pain." This was planned for some performance on the altar without consent from higher authorities and upon discovery of the truth the monks were burned at the stake. Weyer, however, concludes that "perhaps our *Lamiae* sometimes use similar measures on their own bodies."

Myrrh was included in analgesic unguents. Weyer wrote about the use of myrrh in wine. The latter was necessary to make a powder prepared according to Weyer from "gelotophyllis" more acceptable by the patient. This drink caused exhilaration accompanied by endless laughing. He speculated, based on his knowledge of Dioscorides, that a powder prepared from nightshade would have had the same effect. The antidote is "pine wine with the addition of pine-nut kernels and pepper and honey."

The use of pharmaceutical means by the inquisitors in some parts of Europe was commented on earlier in this book. One such recipe from Weyer's *De praestigiis demonum* is as follows, "one dram (1/8 oz.) each of hypericon seed (called 'demon's flight'), frankincense, and carnibenedictum seed. It is offered along with some liquid before the torture begins." It was believed that this mixture compels the accused to confess "any outrage whatsoever."

Herbalism was used to cure diseases throughout Europe during the Middle Ages. Some herbalists, including the midwives, discovered that several plants used in their preparations had magic effects, which unlocked the doors to other perceptions and worlds.

Chapter 4

TOXINS IN PLANTS

> First witch   *"Swelter'd venom sleeping got,*
> *Boil thou first i' the charmed pot.*
> All.   *Double, double toil and trouble;*
> *Fire burn, and, cauldron bubble."*
>
> William Shakespeare, *Macbeth*

The witch picked up plants, collected small animals and cooked them according recipes that were circulated among the practitioners of the art or midwives. Certain plants were used for the witches' preparation in specific proportions, which were very important. A mistake in these proportions turned the ointment into a powerful poison. The witch did not realize, and there was no need for that, what an interesting spectrum of biochemistry riches she had in the cauldron. In fact, it took thousands of scientists to understand some of the substances that were extracted from the witches' plants. Although witches did not care about biochemistry, we could understand how the ointment worked only by analyzing the substances in the witches' cauldron and experimenting.

Poisonous plants and animals were cooked in the witches' cauldron. These plants contained poisons, which are termed toxins today. The term "toxin" is used for the entire spectrum of compound types that are responsible for different toxicoses (condition of poisoning). Toxins range from very simple, small molecules to high molecular weight compounds such as proteins. Plant, animal and fungal toxins cause a number of harmful effects on humans and animals.

Plants and other ingredients used in the witches' ointment, contain various toxins. An important group are the alkaloids. Humans have been using plants containing alkaloids for thousands of years. Sumerian records dating back to 4,000 B.C. describe the effects of opium. The ancient Assyrians, Greeks and Romans used opium for inducing sleep and pain relief. The alkaloids comprise a group of mostly secondary plant compounds. In other words, alkaloids are usually considered to have no major physiological functions for the plant. They have also been found in animals, insects, bacteria, and fungi. Alkaloids are basic nitrogenous compounds. One important of their characteristics is the fact that they form salts with acids. Alkaloids can be classified into three major groups.

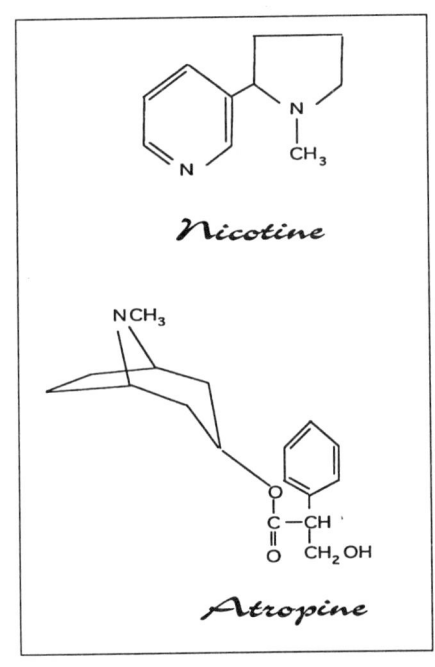

The first one is the group of true alkaloids. The nitrogen atom is in a ring with carbon atoms thus forming a heterocyclic ring.* These alkaloids are derived from amino acid precursors (amino acids are the building blocks of proteins). Examples of this group with physiological effect on man are nicotine found in tobacco and atropine in beladonna.

Plants containing atropine were the most

---

* see Appendix for explanations on presentation of chemical formulae.

important in the preparation of the witches' ointment.
The second group is the group of pseudoalkaloids that are not derived from amino acid precursors. An example is caffeine found in coffee. Mescaline and ephedrine are representatives of the third group of so called protoalkaloids. They have been derived from aminoacids but their nitrogen is not part of a hetrocyclic ring. Mescaline is derived from the hallucinogenic cactus peyote.

Other basic compounds (containing nitrogen) such as cadaverine and histamine are widespread in both plants and animals but they do not belong to the alkaloids. They originate from degradation of other nitrogen containing compounds.

Caffeine

The biochemical isolation and characterization of medicinally effective compounds from plants started at the beginning of the nineteenth century. The first crystalline alkaloid, noscapine, was isolated from opium in 1803. The opium poppy, *Papaver somniferum*, contains also the alkaloid papaverine which exerts a relaxation effect on the human body. Morphine was isolated in 1805 and was named after Morpheus, the Greek god of sleep. Coniine, found in one of the major ingredients of the witches' ointment, poison hemlock, was isolated in 1826 by the pioneers of alkaloid chemistry, Pelletier and Caventou. It was characterized in 1870 and chemically synthesized in 1886.

Today, we know that alkaloid bearing species occur in 34 of the 60 Orders of higher plants. These species represent about 40% of all plant families and about 9% of all genera. Amongst the most important plant families containing alkaloids are the Amaryllidaceae, Compositae, Lauraceae, Leguminosae, Liliaceae, Papaveraceae, Rutaceae, and Solanaceae. All species studied in the Papaveraceae contain alkaloids.

Mescaline

Ephedrine

For this book, the tropane alkaloids are of greatest interest. They are found in some of the plants used for the witches' salve as discussed in the previous chapter and as will be seen further in the book. They are found in the Deadly nightshade, Jimsonweed and Henbane.

Hyoscyamine is the most common alkaloid of the tropane derivatives found in these plants. It is degraded to tropine and tropic acid which do not have the properties of the parent compound. Hyoscyamine is a different form (racemic) of atropine. There are many other alkaloids found in medicinal and hallucinogenic plants from all over the world but these are not within the scope of this book.

Alkaloids are bitter in taste. People have found long time ago that bitter plants were not pallatable and could not be included in their cuisine. In fact, some of these plants were deadly poisons. It is made sure among people living near places where poisonous plants grow that the knowledge of these plants is passed as soon as their children start walking around on their own. Many plants containing alkaloids found their places in herbal medicines all over the world. A selected group of plants were used only by the shamans or oracles in different societies. These were the plants that helped them communicate with the gods.

Alkaloid containing plants affected people's belief in witchcraft in various ways. As an example, some species of lupine (*Lupinus* sp.) as *L. luteus*, *L. albus*, and *L. angustifolius* have been consumed for centuries in European countries. The presence of toxic quinolizidine alkaloids in them hindered their widespread acceptance as a food crop. Lupine seeds were traditionally debbittered to make them good for consumption.

The biosynthesis of the lupine alkaloids occurs in the green parts of the plant, mostly in the leaves. That is also the place where the alkaloids are stored. The seeds are especially rich in alkaloids which are concentrated in the cotyledons.

Other *Lupinus* species as *L. caudatus* (tail cup lupine), *L. sericeus* (silky lupine), and *L. formosus* (Lunara lupine) grew around villages and were grazed by livestock. Laboratory experiments have shown that tail cup lupine, silky lupine and Lunara lupine, as well as poison hemlock, induced gross body abnormalities in livestock. Poison hemlock induced cleft palate in pigs and goats and multiple congenital contractures in pigs, goats, sheep and cattle.

The lupine plants induced cleft palate and multiple congenital contractures in cattle. Some cows fed on these species and gave birth to abnormal babies with limb defects as the one shown on the picture on the following page. Any gross abnormal appearance of animal was scary and considered as a result of Satan's interference. Birth defects were probably thought of as a result of witchcraft. According to many reports of the Inquisition, a burst of witch trials

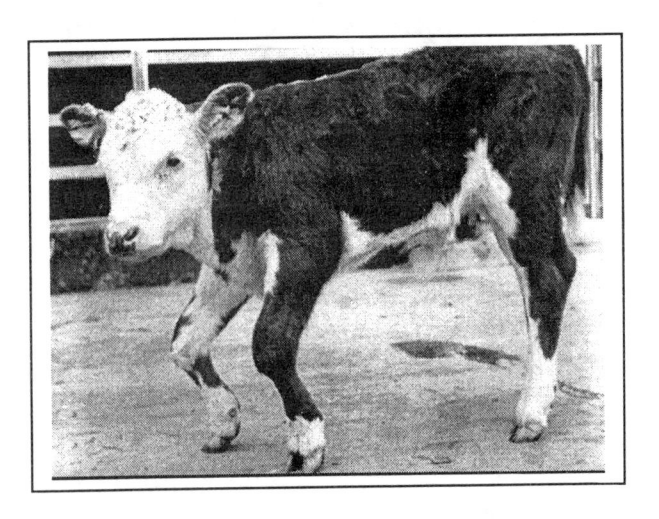

Abnormal calf with a skeletal malformation due to *Lupus* poisoning

began in areas where there were problems with the crops or livestock. Usually such cases were blamed upon some people declared to be in pact with the Evil One. Epidemics among cattle and beasts of burden were also blamed on the local witch. Weyer analyzed such occurrences and absolved the witches from these suspicions. He recommended fumigation with sulfur and other aromatic substances as a cure for the epidemic.

Even nowadays any malformations in animals are considered unwanted and scary. A wave of rebuke exploded on the World Wide Web (www) in 1998 when the cat breeder Vickie Ives Speir posted pictures of her mutant Flipper and her five kittens. Ms Speir's cats had tiny, malformed front legs. "I hope you know that people like you go to hell when they die", wrote an outraged Internet surfer. Ms Spaier received anonymous threats to burn down her home only because she bred cats with limb deformities.

Plant toxins poisoned not only livestock but people too. Some plants used for daily consumption have been considered to affect human pregnancy. Modern scientific results show that cranial defects in newborn babies have been attributed to consumption of lupine or blighted or spoiled potatoes by mothers during pregnancy.

When rye or rye flour is not stored properly in dry places in may be affected by the fungus *Claviceps purpurea.* Its common name is ergot. The ingestion of such flower caused serious forms of gangrene in the Middle Ages. These conditions were known as "St. Anthony's fire." Another form of the disease had symptoms similar to epilepsy, i.e. vilent seizures and lost of consciousness. Ergot was used in popular medicine as an aborting agent. It was widely used by the midwife to hasten birth pangs and in some parts of Europe the procedure was considered witchcraft.

Today, abnormalities in animals and people are the subject of teratology. Teratologists study the reasons for such abnormalities. Scientists have discovered that cleft palate and multiple congenital contractures were induced when pregnant sows ingested alkaloid containing plants. Potato sprouts contain alkaloids which have relative teratogenic potencies.

L. caudatus and *L. sericeus* contain a quinilizidine alkaloid anagyrine believed to be the teratogen. Poison hemlock contains teratogenic piperidine alkaloids. Some scientists are of the opinion that specific chemical structures of the alkaloids are necessary for them to be teratogenic. Many plant genera contain piperidine alkaloids that have such structures. Some of them besides the already mentioned are *Lobelia, Pinus, Punica, Duboisia, Sedum, Liparia* and others. Experiments with sheep and goats showed that in animals fed with *Conium* seed during gestation, the fetal movement was reduced and their kids had severe skeletal abnormalities.

The autumn crocus or meadow saffron (*Colchicum autumnale*) has been responsible for the death of grazing animals. This plant contains colchicine and has been used in medicine since antiquity. It has been used to treat gout and Familial Mediterranean Fever. Many other plants with poisonous characteristics have been useful in treating differen disseases in the past.

Chapter 5

ANIMAL INGREDIENTS

*"Fillet of a fenny snake,
In the cauldron boil and
bake;..."*

William Shakespeare, *Macbeth*, Act IV, Scene I

The pharmacopoeia of the witches consisted of substances predominantly from the plant kingdom, but a few animals or animal parts were also used in the preparation of the ointment. One of the best descriptions of the witches' broth came from Shakespeare's pen in *Macbeth* (Act IV, Scene I). In this poetic recipe most of the ingredients are of animal origin. The literary expression corresponds well to the original recipes, which stagger the imagination. In black magic parts of animal and human corpses were included in their concoctions.

Shakespeare's witches are in a cavern. They are standing around a boiling cauldron and discussing the ingredients of their magic concoction.

First Witch.

*Round about the cauldron go;
In the poison'd entrails throw,-*

Toad*, *that under the cold stone
Days and nights hast thirty-one*

---

* my bold

The inclusion of a toad in the concoction is not for dramatic effect. Toads are poisonous; they have alkaloids, which together with other toxins are used for their protection. These defensive poisons are produced by skin glands. They are constantly secreted in very small amounts and are aimed not only against natural predators but also against microorganisms. Amphibians live in an environment rich in microorganisms. The amphibian skin is moist and is a suitable site for microorganisms and fungi to grow. The researcher Habermehl has shown in his laboratory experiments that these toxins inhibit bacterial and fungal growth.

Amphibian excretions contain various chemical substances. The most important groups are alkaloids, biogenic mines, peptides and steroids. Their pharmacological action is neurotoxic, myotoxic, and hemotoxic. One of the most potent hallucinogens, *o-methyl-bufotenin* is found in an amphibian. The name is derived from the scientific name of the toad (*Bufo alvarius*). Drugs containing this substance, but obtained from trees, are used by South American Indians. The Indians, who lived along the Orinoco River, the frontier between Columbia and Venezuela, used the Yopo snuff. It is prepared from the Anadenanthera seeds, which are first roasted and then ground. The snuff was used to facilitate communication with spirits.

That toads (Common Toads, Bufonidae) are toxic has been known since ancient times. About 3,000 years ago, dried and powdered toad skins were used as heart drugs in Chinese medicine. Such preparations were introduced in Europe in the seventeenth century by traveling merchants. The action of these drugs is equivalent to the glycosides in the Digitalis. Toads, according to mediaeval superstition obtained their toxicity from the poisonous plant Christmas Rose (*Helleborus niger*) because they were frequently found under it. Symptoms of poisoning with this rose are upset stomach and depression. Ingestion of large quantities may cause death. Interestingly, the chemical substance hellebrigenin isolated from the plant is chemically identical to bufotalidin isolated from the toad.

The substances in the toad secretions, which act on the heart as cardiotoxins are, called bufogenines. Their chemical structure was determined in 1949. When bufogenins are chemically linked (to be more precise by an ester bond) with suberylarginine they form the so-called bufotoxins. All these substances cause an increase of the strength of contraction of the heart muscle. The effect is a decrease in the frequency but an increase in the tonus of contractions. Nowadays the *Digitalis* plant is the main source for drugs in heart therapy. Bufogenines and bufotoxins have a very strong anesthetic effect, which might exceed that of cocaine.

Interestingly, the chemist John Daly found a substance in the skin of the frog *Epipedobates tricolor*, which is 200 times more potent than morphine at blocking pain in animals. The substance was named epibatidine after the frog, which is endemic to Equador. However, Daly's efforts to isolate and characterize epibatidine were stymied because laboratory-grown frogs turned out not to make the compound. This reminds us of the old herbalists' rule of thumb that herbs grown in the garden are not as potent as those found in the wild! Dr. Daly could not longer collect the frog in the rainforests of Equador since it had been already included in the threatened species list. About ten years later the chemical structure of epibatidine was determined with nuclear magnetic resonance spectroscopy by using an irreplaceable sample from the rainforest frog's skin, which had been stored in the freezer.

The second witch in Shakespeare's play adds to the cauldron:

"...*Eye of **newt**,* * *and toe of frog,*

---

* my bold

Wool of bat, and tongue of dog,
Addler's fork*, and blind-worm's sting,*
Lizard's leg, and howlet's wing,-
For a charm of powerful trouble,
Like a hell-broth boil and bubble."

Other amphibians used by the witches in their preparation were the newts (genera Tritutrus) and salamanders (genera Salamandra). They belong to the order Urodela. The European Fire Salamander has been known to be toxic since ancient times. In Persian mythology it was described as capable of extinguishing fire. Plinius Secundus (born at Como in 23 A.D.) wrote in his book *Historia Naturalis*, "*Inter omnis venenata, slamandra scelus maximum est*" which translated means "Among all venomous animals, the salamander is the most wicked one." The salamander was a symbol of the alchemists, who tried to convert lead into gold in the medieval times.

Salamanders contain steroid alkaloids, some of which carry their name, i.e. samandarin and samandaridin. Samandarin is a very potent neurotoxin that causes convulsions. Death results from paralysis of the respiratory system. It also possesses very good local anesthetic properties. In the seventeenth century, a German wife cooked a salamander in her soup with the intention of killing her husband. Caught, she was tried and condemned to death for witchcraft. Nowadays, this would be classified as attempted murder with no such serious consequences for the culprit. The secretions of the European newts *T. vulgaris*, *T. alpestris*, *T. marmoratus*, and *T. cristatus* have strong hemolytic* activity.

The addler's fork from the witches' recipe is the tongue of the European viper. People have been aware of the danger of snake bites since the beginning of human history

---

* see Glossary

but the exact cause of death was a mystery. The King of Pontus, Mithridates (123 - 63 B.C.) drank the blood of snakes to become immunized against snake bites, believing that the blood is the carrier of the poison. In 1198 A.D., Maimonides wrote a treatise on poisons but did not explain the origin of snake venom. The Italian physician Francesco Redi (1626-1697 A.D.) wrote a book in 1664 entitled *De venenis Animalibus* and was the first to describe the venom apparatus of snakes. He said that the venom is injected from the venom glands through the teeth, dispelling the idea that other parts of the body were toxic. The tongue of the viper, mentioned by Shakespeare, had probably no efficacious properties in the witches' preparation.

The third witch's contribution;

> *Scale of dragon; tooth of wolf;*
> ***Witches' mummy;*** *maw and gulf*
> *Of the ravin'd salt-sea shark;*
> *Root of hemlock digg'd i' the dark;*
> *Liver of blaspheming Jew;*
> *Gall of goat; and slips of yew*
> *Silvered in the moon's eclipse;*
> ***Nose of Turk**, and Tartar's lips;*
> *Finger of birth-strangled babe*
> *Ditch deliver's by a drab-*
> *Make the gruel thick and slab;*
> *And thereto a **tiger's chaudron**,*
> *For the ingredients of our cauldron.*

All.   *Double, double toil and trouble;*
       Fire burn, and, cauldron bubble.

Second Witch.

> *Cool it with a baboon's blood,*
> *Then the charm is firm and good.*

Shakespeare's "included" a part of a witch's mummy in the broth was because mummies were valued as precious merchandise in the Orient during his time probably due to the aromatics used in the embalming procedure. However, the availability of mummies to European witches is more than questionable.

It should be noted that that the art of embalming was considered as a sorcery itself. Any documentary evidence on embalming in the old Kingdom of Pharaonic Egypt (2660-2180 B.C.) is missing. The embalmers had to swear an oath not to tell the secret of embalming techniques to anybody. Today's technology made it possible to analyze the conservation techniques and the ointments used in embalming. The analysis of the mummified skeleton of Idu II, secretary general of the pine wood trade office who lived circa 2200 B.C. (see http://mfah.org/splendor/docs/highlts/hildemus.html), showed the presence of cyclic alcohols, including cedrol, gujacol, *tert*-octylphenol, trymethyl-cyclohexene methanol, and actahydronaphthalene methanol. These volatile products originate from the liquid fraction of wood tar and are well known for their inhibitory action on bacterial and fungal growth. The presence of these compounds, as well as diterpenoid resin acids, indicates that the skeleton of the Idu mummy was possibly flamed with a tar-rich torchlight. The corpse of the secretary general of the pine wood trade office was defleshed and then wrapped up.

The contribution of a "nose of Turk" to the witches' ointment is very doubtful, too. Any one's nose in this preparation regardless of nationality is not a very appealing idea.

The "tiger's chaudron" refers to the entrails of the tiger which is highly prized in Chinese medicine. The animal is recognized as endangered species. Monetary pressure forces the poachers to kill these animals to extinction. Almost all tiger's body parts are valued. A bowl of soup of male tiger's sexual organs costs between $200-

350. This soup is believed to give longevity and sexual vitality.

As defined previously, an ointment is a preparation in which the active ingredient or a drug is carried to the target system in the body by a substance, called a vehicle. The vehicle in the witches' ointment was animal grease of various origins. The First Witch from Shakespeare's *Macbeth* used the following as a vehicle in their unguent:

> *" Pour in sow's blood, that hath eaten*
> *Her nine farrow;* **grease** *that's sweaten*
> *From the murderer's gibbet throw*
> *Into the fame."*

The fat that drops from the body of the chained murderer was a precious substance highly valued in the Middle Ages. In 1404 A.D., the Parliament in Paris was occupied with cases in which corpses of criminals were stolen from the gallows to be used in witchcraft.

Anne-Marie de Georgel, whose trial in the fourteenth century was discussed previously in the book, confessed that she obtained ingredients (clothing, hair, nails, and fat) for the ointments from cemeteries and gallows. This activity is recorded for the first time in her case. In the work of an anonymous Savoyard Inquisitor entitled *Errores Gazariorum* published about 1450 A.D., the fat of a hanged man was used in the preparation of the ointment.

Human fat was long believed to be a remedy for rheumatism and sprains. The fat of a stillborn baby, however, was the one mentioned most often in diabolical texts. A poetic description of the horrid recipe could be obtained from Shadwell's play of the Lancashire Witches. Mother Demdike says:

> *"Oyntment for flying here I have,*
> *Of children's fat stoln from the grave,*
> *The juice of smallage and nightshade,*
> *Of poplar-leaves and aconite made;..."*

Usually the baby fat was highly valued by the supposed witches. This fat was also believed to be necessary in medications against leprosy. It is suggested that in such cases midwifes were involved in procuring the material. The midwife Perrette, spouse of Thomas of Rouen, was involved in finding a source of such fat.

In his book *The Discoverie of Witchcraft*, Reginald Scot (1584 A.D.) also reported about the popular belief of using baby's fat:

> "**Rx** *The fat of yoong children, and seeth it with water in a brasen vessel and serving the thickest of that which remaineth boiled in the bottome, which they laie up and keepe, until occasion severth to use it...*"

The use of infant fat was driven by superstition and not by a real value of the material. Fat was only a vehicle for the drugs contained in the ointments, which were mainly of plant origin. The origin of the fat did not increase the efficacy of the unguent in anyway. This is supported by the opinion of some apothecaries from the mediaeval period who considered the fat of an unbaptized child as no better than a goose-grease or pig fat. Another source of fat as mentioned in the trial accounts at Todi in 1428 A.D. was a vulture, whose fat was mixed with babies' blood. Cat and dog fat was also used for ointments. Such fat has been recommended in old herbal ointment recipes. Herbalists recommend pig's lard as the best vehicle in ointment preparations.

Chapter 6
HERBS USED IN THE FLYING OINTMENT

"Where be the magical herbs?
Hecate

They are down his throat;
His mouth cramm'd full, his ears and nostrils stuff'd;
I thrust in eleoselium lately,
Aconitum, frondes populeas, and soot-
You may see that, he looks so black in the mouth-
Then sium, acorum vulgare too,
Pentaphyllon, the blood of a flitter-mouse,
Solanum somnificum et oleum."

Middleton, *The Witch*

Most of the plants that were used as ingredients in the witches' ointment are **poisonous**. Their herbal histories are much older than the Middle Ages. Although they have been used medicinally for centuries, nowadays they are not recommended for home use, and publications of recipes including these plants are discouraged for safety reasons. Several of the plants discussed in this book are used in controlled preparation of drugs. Their medicinal use should be conducted after physician's recommendation and advice only.

Herbs that represent the major constituents of the witches' ointment are listed below. They have been grouped according to the planet, which rules them, following the classification of the English Mediaeval herbalist Culpeper. Despite scientific attempts to explain the biochemical basis of herbal use in treatment of various diseases, the celestial link to plants and animals is not to be underestimated. A careful study of the influence of planets on every plant and living creature will be rewarding for the student of herbalism and the Art of ointment preparation.

Saturn

Saturn rules Capricorn (December 22- January 20) and affects bones, knees, teeth, vagus nerve, and some pituitary hormones in man. Astrologers characterize Saturn as cold and wicked. John of Salisbury wrote in his book *Policraticus* in 1159 A.D. that Saturn "spares from harm scarcely the astrologers themselves." It is noteworthy that the most important plants used in the preparation of the ointment are under the dominion of Saturn.

Aconitum napellus (Ranunculaceae)

A legend tells us, that *Aconitum* came from the hill of Aconitus where the monstrous three headed dog Cerberus, a child of the serpent woman Echidna and Typhon, was killed by Hercules. The saliva of the monster became the deadly poison of the plant. Hecate, the Greek goddess of the moon, ghosts, witches, and magic, poisoned her father with the herb.

This plant is known as common Monkshood, libbard's-bane, leopard's-bane and Aconite. Pliny, the author of *Naturalis Historia* was of the opinion that the name *Aconitum* was derived from the Black Sea port of Aconis. Other writers believed it evolved from the Greek word akoniton (akoniton), from *akon* which means a dart. This is probably explained by the fact that the root juice was used to make poisonous arrows.

The Monkshood is an herbaceous perennial which overwinter as a stout black root very similar to turnip in shape. The stem is usually 50-150 cm* tall. It carries dark green palmate leaves, each with 5-7 toothed main lobes. The hooded flowers are dark blue to dark violet. They could be seen from June to September.

The plant, found in shady places, prefers damp ground in the hilly regions of the country. Native to Europe and temperate Asia, it was also imported to North America by the early settlers.

Monkshood contains the alkaloid aconitine, which is found in the root, leaves and flowers. Monkshood is thought to be the most poisonous flowering plant in Europe. Poisoning occurs when it has been confused with other plants and the leaves used in salads or dishes. Even picking the flowers might cause tingling in the skin and numbness.

The yellow *Aconitum vulparia* (syn. *A. lycotonum*), listed as Wolfsbane, has pale green leaves and pale yellow flowers. It is also very poisonous containing the same alkaloid as *A. napelus*. This plant has been used "since classical times as a sure method to dispose of unwanted spouse...", according to Culpeper. A plant related to the European Aconite that grows in India is *Aconitum ferox*. It contains the alkaloid pseudo-aconitine, which is also a powerful poison.

Aconitine affects the proper conduction of nerve impulses, this resulting in failure to coordinate the movements of the body. Within 10-20 minutes after ingestion, one feels a burning sensation in the mouth and throat. This sensation spreads all over the body (including the skin) and is accompanied by sweating. The victim has the peculiar feeling that his hands are made of fur, described as the "glove feeling." Then, cold sweats follow and cause a feeling of deathly chill over the whole body. Accompanying symptoms are: nausea, vomiting, diarrhea, and pains in the head, neck, back and heart region. Singing in the ears is experienced together with disturbances in vision. Death

---

*see Abbreviations

occurs very suddenly (within 30 minutes to 3 hours) through circulatory paralysis and cardiac arrest.

The properties of *Aconitum* plants have been known through the ages and considered as "vulgar poisons." An exception was the custom on the ancient Greek island of Cos where a draught of Aconite was officially recognized as a legitimate way of putting an end to the life a person who had reached the old age. The Roman Emperor Trajan forbade the growing of Aconitum by law and punished by death.

Aconite is connected with the career of Pier Andrea Mattioli, one of the most famous herbalists of the sixteenth century. He was a physician to the Roman Emperor but his true fame came with the publication of his commentaries on Dioscorides. He is remembered also with for his experimentation with condemned criminals to determine if the Monkshood was more poisonous than other aconites.

Commentators suggest that the poison which the Apothecary sold to Romeo in Shakespeare's *Romeo and Juliet* was Aconite. In Act V, Scene 1. Romeo says:

> *Hold, there is forty ducats: let me have*
> *A dram of poison; such soon-speeding gear*
> *As will disperse itself through all the veins,*
> *That the life-weary taker may fall dead,*
> *And that the trunk may be discharged of breath*
> *As violently as hasty powder fired*
> *Doth hurry from the fatal cannon's womb.*

The Apothecary sold him a substance worth his money:

> *Put this in any liquid thing you will,*
> *And drink it off; and, if you had the strength*
> *Of twenty men, it would dispatch you straight.*

This terrible poison, however, used in small quantities and with caution brings blessed relief from pain.

The physicians of Myddvai in Wales in the thirteenth century thought that the Monkshood should be known and used by every physician. It was used in to treat acute neuralgias, painful diseases in the joints, and also for pneumonias. The best extracts were prepared by making a tincture of one pound of Aconite and a quart of alcohol which was then evaporated. According to the authorities of the time, overdoses should be avoided for no antidote was known.

Culpeper recommended a decoction of the root for washing the parts of the body bitten by venomous creatures. The shoot of the plant "is very serviceable against vegetable poisons." This property was used by the witches and is discussed further in the book.

Atropa belladonna (Solanaceae)

The plant is known as Deadly Nightshade but in some places the names Naughty man's Cherries, Black Cherry, Banewort, Dwayberry, Divale and Dwale are also used. It is native to central and southern Europe, North Africa and some regions of Asia. The Nightshade is found also in North America.

The generic name of the species reflects its evil nature. It comes from Greek mythology. The three goddesses of fate were Clotho, Lachesis, and Atropos. Clotho spanned life's thread when men were born. Her sister, Lachesis determined its length. Atropos was the sister responsible for cutting off the thread of human life. She used the berries of the plant to fulfill her duties. Belladonna was the plant's common name but later it became its specific name. Meaning beautiful lady, it refers to the practice of women putting drops in their eyes to dilate the pupils and make them more attractive.

Belladonna was the most important plant on the list of the witchcraft pharmacopoeia in Medieval Europe. Nightshade was known to promote madness and hallucinations and therefore called Devil's Herb (Cherry), Sorcerer's Herb and Apple of Sodom.

A Prussian pastor described the use of belladonna for murder by Lithuanians, who called it *mauled*, in the 17th century. When they owned money to someone they would find a way to introduce the poison in his drink. "Whoever receives this plant into his body must die; the whole pharmacopoeia cannot help him," says an old text.

The Nightshade contains the alkaloid atropine, which has a paralyzing effect in small doses. The alkaloid is found throughout the plant, i.e. leaves, roots, flowers and berries. As few as three berries are sufficient to kill a very small child. The poison of the plant might be absorbed through the skin. Human poisoning has been reported after eating rabbits and birds that have fed on the plant.

A large amount of atropine produces excitation of the nervous system. The victim experiences euphoria and becomes talkative and excited. Laughter and dancing may accompany this behavior which soon becomes uncontrollable. Phantoms and movements start appearing before him, and music sounds in his ears. The victim is entirely confused and as the German scientist Schenck[*] writes "he is completely open to influence and will do whatever he is told."

Other clinical symptoms of nightshade poisoning are: fever, rapid pulse, dilation of pupils, hot and dry skin. If a

---

[*] see Bibliography for references

fatal dose of the poison has been taken, the temperature suddenly falls and death occurs. It is caused due to paralysis of the respiratory center.

A method to diagnose Beladonna poisoning requires that a few drops of urine from the subject are applied to a cat's eye. Exposure to light after 30 minutes will cause dilation of the cat's pupils if belladonna has been ingested. The alkaloid atropine from the ingested plant would be present in the urine and would cause the dilation of the pupils.

In Culpeper's *Complete herbal* the Deadly Nightshade is not assigned to any planet but according to him the Common Nightshade is under the dominion of Saturn.

Cicuta virosa (**Umbelliferae**)

This umbelliferous plant is known as water hemlock, cowbane, poison parsnip, carotte a moreau, or beaver poison. It grows beside the ponds and marshes of Europe. Six species of *Cicuta* are known to grow in North America.

The blossom is composed of partial umbels. The roots have the taste of carrot or parsley. They smell like celery. The water hemlock is extremely dangerous for it might be picked by children or ignorant people and will poison them. The stem was used throughout the bucolic period of Ancient Greece and the antique world for making

$$HOCH_2 - (CH_2)_2 - (C \equiv C)_2 - \underset{OH}{CH} - (CH_2)_2 - CH_3$$

Cicutoxin

the Pan pipes. Gustav Schenk commented thus: "Thus the

selfsame plant that causes man a horrible death provided the musical instrument from which all Western music is derived. This is a strangely poignant thought."

All organs of the water hemlock contain cicutoxin, considered the most terrifying and dramatic in its operation poison. Its content is especially high in the tubers. After 20 minutes to an hour after ingestion, the mouth and throat begin to burn. The victim feels nausea, palpitation and abdominal pains. These symptoms are accompanied by a paradoxical feeling of intoxication, but quite different from alcohol intoxication. A brief faint usually occurs which " a prelude to the real process of destruction." After the collapse, the sufferer is seized by terrible convulsions, accompanied by screams and vomiting. These convulsions are very much like epileptic fits with the accompanying grinding of the teeth. "It is life in the Inferno, however, life in the hemlock hell," as Schenk commented. The seizures recur time after time at 15 minute intervals. Death occurs a few hours after ingestion but these hours are full of agony.

Conium maculatum (**Umbelliferae**)

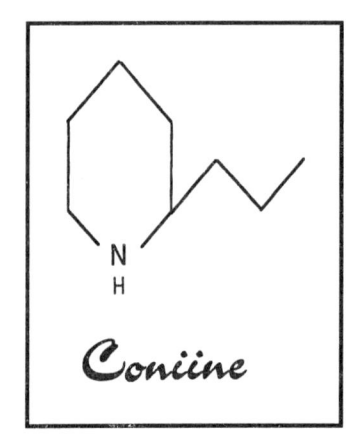

The plant is known as (spotted) hemlock. It grows along the edges of woods, in hedges, extending up into the mountains of Europe and parts of Asia. It is now naturalized in North America. All parts of the plant contain the alkaloid coniine and about four other alkaloids as well as ethereal oils.

We know about the lethal effects of hemlock through Plato's description of Socrates' execution. Socrates was one of the great philosophers of ancient Greece. His philosophy was based on a method of asking a series of questions which would lead you to the truth. When his young followers started asking questions about authority, the men in power became alarmed and sentenced the philosopher to death. Socrates was given a cup of hemlock draught, drank it and died in 399 B.C. It is clear from Plato's careful account that Socrates was poisoned with spotted hemlock and not water hemlock (see below). The plant is so poisonous that even blowing a whistle made of its stem causes poisoning.

The ancient Roman name for hemlock was Cicuta. The name was used in the Latin literature probably until the middle of the sixteenth century when Gesner and other writers used it for the Water Hemlock (*Cicuta virosa*) which is described below. In 1737 A.D., Linnaeus in his system of classification, called the spotted hemlock *Conium maculatum* to avoid confusion. The new generic name of Conium came from the Greek word *koneion* (κονειον), which means to spin or whirl. This referred to the disastrous effects of the plant on the human body when it was eaten. Maculatum means spotted or speckled.

Hemlock, has probably been used since the Anglo-Saxon period. It was known as *Hemlic* or *Hymelic* derived from the word *healm* for straw. The word *leac* for leek or plant came from the dry and hollow stems of the plant after it had flowered.

It is a biennial or perennial plant. The stem is hollow and 1-2 m tall with purplish-red spots on the lower part. The tap root is spindle shaped and white in color. It has an odor like that of parsnip and has often been mistaken for it. The leaves are dark-green to gray green, pinnately decompound and carried on round stalks. They resemble parsley in appearance and for that reason the spotted hemlock is mistaken with parsley. The Poison Hemlock has also similar leaves and flowers to these of the wild carrot (*Daucus carota*, Queen Anne's Lace). The wild carrot has hairy leafstalks in contrast to the Poison Hemlock; the carrot stem is also hairy and branching, while the Spotted Hemlock has a hairless, purple-mottled stem.

The flowers of Poison Hemlock are small, white, borne in umbels with 10-20 rays. They appear in June to September. The seeds are greenish-brown and ovate, with wavy ribs and 3 mm long and are often mistaken with the seeds of anise. During hot summer days one can recognize the area where hemlock grows by the repugnant smell reminiscent of mouse urine.

At first coniine acts by excitation and later by depression of the spinal cord and the part of the brain called *medulla oblongata* or brain stem. About 30 minutes to 2 hours after ingestion, the victim suffers from burning sensation in the mouth, difficulty in swallowing, excessive salivation, disturbance of the vision and weakness in the limbs. The pupils become dilated. There might be vomiting and diarrhea. Death is due to respiratory failure. Records show that the philosopher Socrates died of general paralysis, which corresponds to the described symptoms.

During the Middle Ages the bitter juice of hemlock was taken only for "the bite of mad dogge" against rabies. It was mixed with Betony and Fennel seed in wine and taken orally. It was known that hemlock could be safely used externally in ointments and poultices. These were applied for inflammations, indolent tumors, swellings. The monks of the fifteenth and sixteenth centuries used roasted hemlock roots for relieving the pains of gout and applied it not only to the painful parts, but also to their hands and wrists. In the 1760s it began to be used by Stoerck, a physician and author of medicinal books, as a cure for cancerous ulcers.

According to Culpeper the best antidote for the Hemlock, if too much of the herb is taken, is pure wine. The plant is under the dominion of Saturn.

Hyoscyamus niger (Solanaceae)

This is the black henbane, which might be easily found in places where man has dumped garbage or around cemeteries. Schenck writes that "this sinister-looking plant seems to live on human refuse, on the corpses in the cemetery or the offal that lies around human dwellings. Black henbane seems to suck up and retain within it all the poisonous matter from its habitat."

The use of this plant dates back to ancient Greece. The generic name *Hysoscyamus* evolved from the Greek *hyoskyamos,* with *hys* meaning hog, and *kyamos*, bean. Doiscorides wrote that since pigs could eat the poisonous seed the plant had been named Hog's bean. The specific name of *niger*, meaning black, referred to the parts of the human body that turned black and rotted when the plant extracts were applied to them (necrosis). The Anglo-Saxons knew the plant as Belene, which described probably its bell-shaped flowers.

The herb was used for the production of the Soporific Sponges in old times. It was administered to patients before painful operations such as amputations. Dioscorides prescribed henbane as a procurer of sleep and pain reliever.

Shakespeare knew about the properties of henbane and used it as the means of murder of Hamlet's father (Hamlet, Act I, Scene V). The ghost of the murdered King reveals the true story about his death to Hamlet:

> *Brief let me be. Sleeping within my orchard,*
> *My custom always of the afternoon,*
> *Upon my secure hour thy uncle stole,*
> *With juice of **cursed hebenon**[*] in a vial,*
> *And in the porches of my ears did pour*
> *The leperous distilment; whose effect*
> *Holds such an enmity with blood of man*

---

[*] my bold

That swift as quicksilver it courses through
The natural gates and alleys of the body,
And with a sudden vigor it doth posset
And curd, like eager droppings into milk,
The thin and wholesome blood.....

Henbane is an erect annual or biennial herb with hairy stems 30-150 cm long. It has gray oblong leaves with a few coarse teeth, not stalked. The plant has yellowish flowers veined with purple which are in the leaf axils and five-lobed. The fruit is a rounded capsule enclosed by a five lobe calyx.

The black henbane contains the alkaloids hyoscyamine, hyoscine, and atropine in all its organs. Its use is usually accompanied by temporary memory loss. It is difficult for the victim of henbane poisoning to recollect what has happened. This is quite the opposite of the recollections after the use of the Mexican peyote cactus. Under the influence of this cactus all the experiences are recalled.

Michael Schenck's personal experience with black henbane is as follows: "The henbane's first effect was purely physical discomfort. My limbs lost certainty, pains hammered in my head, and I began to feel extremely giddy....I went to the mirror and was able to distinguish my face, but more dimly than normal. It looked flushed and must have been so. I had the feeling that my head had increased in size: it seemed to have grown broader, more solid heavier, and I imagined that it was enveloped in firmer, thicker skin. The mirror itself seemed to be swaying, and I found it difficult to keep my face within its frame. The black discs of my pupils were immensely enlarged, as though the whole iris, which was normally blue, had become black. Despite of the dilation of my pupils I could see no better than usual; quite the contrary, the outlines of objects were hazy, the window and the window frame were obscured by a thin mist."

Schenck's pulse became rapid and he experienced further all the hallucinatory power of the plant. "There were animals which looked at me keenly with contorted grimaces and staring, terrified eyes; there were terrifying stones and clouds of mist, all sweeping along in the same direction. They carried me irresistibly with them. Their coloring must be described - but it was not a pure hue. They enveloped in a vague gray light, which emitted a dull glow and rolled onward and upward into a black and smoky sky. I was flung into a flaring drunkenness, a witches' cauldron of madness. above my head water was flowing, dark and blood-red. The sky was filled with herds of animals. Fluid, formless creatures emerged from the darkness. I heard words, but they were all wrong and nonsensical, and yet they possessed for me some hidden meaning."

The effects of the black henbane as experienced above will be described again later in the book but this time they refer to an ointment prepared by a German enthusiast who used an old witches' recipe. Although he did not list the ingredients used, it will become obvious that the black henbane was a major component.

In folk medicine, leaves of the black henbane (*Folia Hysosciami*) are used for inflammation of the ear and earaches. They are cooked 15 to 20 minutes below simmering, in vegetable oil. The herbs are strained and a few drops of the preparation are used. It is understandable, that if you increase the strength of the preparation, the medicine turns into a poison. That is what Hamlet's uncle took advantage of to kill his own brother and become a King.

Lolium temulentum

Darnel is a common weed seen in the fields. The plant was believed to be among the favorites of the Devil and used by witches in their concoctions. Darnel was reported to cause blindness. According to Culpeper. It had a cleansing effect on the skin against leprosy, when used with salt and radish roots. Darnel is not recommended enthusiastically by herbalists nowadays.

Populus spp. (Salicaceae)

The Black poplar is a tree found in the woods of Europe and Asia. Poplar leaves were listed in Jiovani Batista's recipe for the witches' ointment. The leaves of the Black Poplar were applied with vinegar for gout problems in the Middle Ages. The juice of the White Poplar leaves was used for earaches. Nowadays, the buds of the tree are used for medicinal purposes. They contain the phenol glucosides salicin and populin. The buds are used for the preparation of salve for external use on wounds and hemorrhoids.

Plants have been grouped on the basis of content of active compounds and their use in oral hygiene all over the world due to their appealing flavor. Poplar leaves are to be found in group #5. Besides the glucosides listed above, they contain other anti-inflammatory substances as cinnamic acid, a-d-bisabolol, and trichocarpin. The Native Americans used *Populus* for teeth cleaning. Today, the tree is used for production of commercial tooth-picks and as the source of buds in cough medicine.

The poplar was known since antiquity. According to *Genesis* (30:37-43), Jacob won a bet from his father-in-law with the help of a poplar tree. Jacob was promised all the mottled and striped goats from his father-in-law's herd. Animals of such color were rare and Jacob's father-in-law was sure he would not lose. Jacob placed an arrangement of striped rods made from the poplar, almond, and plane trees before the breeding animals. With God's help, this approach worked and most of the baby-goats were mottled or striped. Jacob won the bet.

The Greek hero Hercules wore a crown of poplar leaves when he fought the three-headed dog Cerberus.

During this fight the leaves were burned by the fumes of Hades and that is the reason the poplar leaves are darker green on the top side.

Jupiter

This planet rules Sagitarius (November 23 - December 21) and governs fats, liver, ears, arterial system and blood.

Datura stramonium (Solanaceae)

The Thornapple can be found throughout the temperate regions of Europe, Asia and North America. It grows usually in vacant lots and rubbish dumps. Other names used for it are Jamestown weed, Jimsonweed, Stinkweed, Datura.

The plant has a bad reputation that came from the early periods of Indian and Russian history. Thieves used to grind the seeds, mix them with water and give them to the intended victims before robbing them. A similar recipe was used by the members of an ancient Indian religious organization, called "thugs", who killed in the service of the Destruction Goddess Kali. The generic name of the Thornapple, Datura is mentioned in some early Sanskrit writings as *dhustura* or *dhatura.*

Ancient Chinese doctors prescribed the plant and other related species under the name *man-to-lo* for the sedative effects. In Chianese Pharmacopoeia the dry flowers of *Datura metel* are officially prescribed and used as spasmolytic, antiasmathic and anesthetic treatment. The priests of Apollo at Delphi in ancient Greece took small amounts of the leaves to get inspiration during the ritual of prophecy making.

In 38 B.C. soldiers from the Roman Emperor Antony's army ate some of the plant while retreating from the battlefield and lost control of their senses. The same thing happened with American soldiers near Jamestown in 1676. As a result of this, the plant became known as Jamestown weed which evolved into Jimson weed.

The use of *Datura* for smoking was probably introduced to medieval Europe by gypsies who brought it from India. They smoked it to experience hallucinations.

Datura is a large (up to 1.5 m tall) annual with a green to purplish stem, wide branching near the tip. The leaves are alternate, simple, ovate-elliptic and 7-20 cm long. The fruit is a dry, ovoid capsule bearing sharp prickles.

All parts of the plant contain the alkaloids hyoscyamine, atropine, and hyoscine (scopolamine). The seeds and the leaves are particularly rich with these alkaloids. I should point out once again that the witches' salve effect was based mainly on the thornapple and henbane extracts.

A seventeenth century account of the "black madness" describes the symptoms of thornapple poisoning: "The servants ate of a dish of lentils into which thornapple seeds had accidentally come. Afterwards they all became foolish. The lacemaker worked with unusual diligence, throwing the bobbin vigorously to and fro but getting everything into a frightful muddle. The chambermaid came into the room shouting at the top of her voice, 'Look, all the devils from hell are coming in!' One servant carried the wood piece by piece into the secret chamber, announcing that he must burn brandy there. Another struck two hatches of wood axes together, saying that he had to chop up wood. Another crawled about on all fours scratching up grass and earth with his mouth and grubbing about in it like a pig with its snout. Yet another imagined himself a cartwright and wanted to bore holes in every piece of wood he could lay his hands on. Afterwards he took a big piece of wood in which a large hole had been bored, held this hole to his mouth as if he was drinking and the said: 'I've hardly begun to get drunk. Oh, what a wonderful drink this is!' Thus the good fellow had imagined himself to be drinking from an empty hole through a piece of dry wood. Another went into the smithy and called out for people to come and help him catch fish, for there were huge shoals of fish swimming in the smithy. To others this fool's plant gave other crazy ideas, so that they engaged in all kinds of labour without being paid for it and acted a proper comedy. The next day none of them knew what ludicrous antics they had got up to. Not one of them would believe or allow himself to be persuaded that he had had these fantasies."

Besides the effects on the nervous system described above, thornapple poisoning with higher doses is accompanied by thirst, pupil dilation, dry mouth, redness of the skin, nausea, rapid pulse, headache, high temperature and high blood pressure. It might result in convulsions, coma or death.

Children have been poisoned by the sap of the plant. The leaves of Jimson weed used by mistake in "tea" could be fatal. Even as 4-5 grams of leaves (or seeds) could poison a small child. The nasty nature of the plant is demonstrated by the fact that a family in Tennessee grafted tomato plants onto Jimson weed roots in order to obtain larger and harder tomatoes than the usual harvest but got intoxicated after they consumed the tomatoes.

Some indications of a teratogenic effect of *Datura* after consumption by pigs were reported in Kansas, USA. This has been questioned, however, by later studies.

A greater variety of *Datura* species has been found in The New World than in Europe. They have been used through the centuries by ancient cultures as medicinal, as well as ritual plants during religious ceremonies. The ancient civilization of Mohica might have used *Datura arborea* to calm maniacal individuals. The Mohica lived in the north coastal area of Peru from 100 B.C. until about 700 A.D. The Mexican species *Datura ceratocaula* grows in marshes and shallow waters. It was considered by the Aztecs a holy medicine and was respectfully addressed before used.

Another ancient culture on the south coast of Peru (circa A.D. 100-800), called the Nazka, also used *Datura* species during their ceremonies. A motif on their ceramics suggests the use of *Datura floripondio*. The most important Datura species for the Aztecs used in ceremonies was *Datura inoxia*, the famous Toloache of Mexico. Nowadays, its roots, seeds, and leaves are added to tesquino, a ceremonial drink used by the modern Tarahumara of Mexico.

A step by step record of experiments with Datura under the guidance of a Yaqui sorcerer is described in Carlo Castaneda's book *The teachings of Don Juan: a Yaqui way of knowledge*. The plant, together with the cactus peyote (*Lophophora williamsii*) and a variety of the mushroom species *Psylocibe* was used during the initial stage of Castaneda's initiation in the sorcerers' art. In an interview, Castaneda elaborated that the use of these plants was necessary to "stop the flow of ordinary interpretations." He further stated that the drugs alone did not help you to "stop the world," a conclusion true also for the effects of the ointment – pharmacology is not always the greatest tool.

Commiphora (Bursaraceae)

Plants that were not native to Europe but which gave the highly valued product myrrh in the Old Continent, are several shrubs of the genus *Commiphora* of the Burseraceae. An Egyptian papyrus dated about 2000 B.C. is one of the earliest records of man's use of myrrh.

An ancient Syrian myth, later adopted by the Greeks, tells us that Myrrha, the daughter of the Syrian King Thesis, was punished by the goddess because she did not respect Ahprodite's feelings. She was forced to commit incest with

Furanoeudesma-1,3-diene

her father. With the assistance of her nurse, Myrrha disguised herself and deceived Thesis for eleven nights. On the twelfth night he discovered the trick and became furious. He started chasing her with a knife with the intention of killing her. The gods were merciful and transformed her into the myrrh tree. Her tears are the clear resin that drops from the wounded myrrh plant.

Myrrh is a natural compound secreted by these plants and is composed of essential oils, water soluble gums and alcohol-soluble resins. It contains sesquiterpenes, which are responsible for the pain-killing virtues of the compound. The sesquiterpenes interact with opioid receptors in the brain membrane. As mentioned earlier, myrrh was used with wine as an analgesic. No evidence exists for its use by witch trial victims although its characteristics were well known throughout Europe.

Venus

Venus rules Taurus (April 21-May 21) and Libra (September 24-October 23). This planet has control over throat, chin, complexion, hair, kidneys, and generative systems. Emotions are influenced by Venus.

Digitalis purpurea (Schrophulariaceae)

The Anglo-Saxons called this and other species of the *Digitalis* genus *foxes glofa*, which meant the glove of the fox. Another name used was *foxes gleow*. *Gleow* is a mediaeval instrument consisting of many bells. The botanical name was given to the plant by the German herbalist Fuch. It is derived from the Latin word *digitus*, meaning finger, referring to the shape of the flowers. The German name is *Fingerhut*, a finger hat or thimble. The species name *purpurea* describes the purple color of the flowers. Other names used for this plant are Purple Foxglove, Dead Man's bells, Bloody Fingers, Gloves of our Lady and Witches Thimbles.

The Purple Foxglove is a native to Europe. It is planted in the United States and Hawaii as a garden ornamental plant. It is also naturalized in some areas of the United States.

The Foxglove is a biennial herb with alternate, simple and toothed leaves. The flowers are in a terminal raceme and tubular to 7-8 cm long. The fruit is a dry capsule.

The ancient Druids are known to have used the Foxglove and valued its medicinal properties. The thirteenth century physicians of Myddvai in Wales used the leaves as external medicine. Dodoens (1544 A.D.) prescribed Foxglove for internal used after boiling the leaves in wine. This remedy poisoned a lot of people. The mashed leaves or juice in the form of ointment were used for swellings and ulcers. According to Culpeper, the Italians applied the plant leaves onto wounds.

Mahatma Ghandi used to sip tea brewed from the leaves of the plant. Holy men have been known to chew it while meditating. The use of the plant in this way is not recommended. Children might get poisoned from sucking the attractive flowers or eating the leaves or seeds. Symptoms include nausea, diarrhea, stomach pain, sever headache. This accompanied by irregular heartbeat and pulse, tremors, convulsions and death. An antidote is atropine.

Verbena officinalis (Verbenaceae)

Vervain is included both in the witches' pharmacopoeia and in the list of plants used against witches. The plant is considered as a principal ingredient of the witches' ointment by various authors. Vervain was used in some demonological practices. Anyone who tries to enter into communication with demons must be enclosed by the magical circle under penalty of certain death. There are various diagrams for the circle in sorcerers' manuscripts from the medieval period. In a book of magic dated 1522 (but in fact printed in 1822), the operator, called "karcist", stands in a small circle. There are two candles on either side, which are placed in wreaths of vervain.

According to Culpeper vervain is 'excellent for the womb.' The herb was used by the midwife in her practices during Mediaeval times.

Sorrels

In 1698 A.D., a young Irish girl gave some bread and beer to a begging old woman. The story goes further and tells us that the girl put a leaf of sorrel in her mouth, which was given to her by the witch. The girl was seized later with convulsions and lost consciousness. After the girl came to herself she started vomiting different things. Her seizures stopped only after the old woman was arrested and taken to a great distance from the home of the girl.

From the story it is not clear what kind of sorrel was given to the girl but Sheep's Sorrel (*Rumex acetosella*), Common Sorrel (*R. acetosa*) and Moutain Sorrel (*Oxyria digyna*, syn. *O. reniformis*) are edible plants. The Sheep's Sorrel is an annual growing to about 30 cm high. It has narrow sharp-pointed leaves. Later in the spring it develops stalks clustered with green flowers which turn into red. The name Sorrel comes from the French *sur*, which stands for sour. The species name *acetosella* means "little vinegar plant." These names reflect the sour taste of the plant. The leaves are used in salads and are also used to make Sorrel soup in the French cuisine.

The problem with the Irish girl might be explained if instead of a Sorrel leaf, she put in her mouth a leaf from the Climbing (Deadly) Nightshade (*Solanum dulcamara*). Sorrel grows sometimes alongside the Deadly Nightshade. Both plants have arrow shaped leaves. However, the Deadly Nightshade has purple flowers, red berries and is a vine, whereas Sorrel is an upright herbaceous plant. The Deadly Nightshade contains the glyco-alkaloid solanine. The symptoms of poisoning are headache, stomach ache, paralysis, shock, respiratory depression and vomiting. All the above symptoms describe the condition of the young girl. Whether by mistake or on purpose, the girl was probably poisoned. Poisoning in the Middle Ages was equivalent to bewitching and the old woman was executed.

Mercury

This planet rules Gemini (May 22- June 21) and Virgo (the Virgin; August 24 - September 23). Brain, intellect, mental perception, thyroid gland, nervous system are influenced by Mercury.

Mandragora officinarum

Known as mandrake or mandragora (not to be confused with the "mandrake root" which is *Podophyllum pelatum,* also known as the May Apple) it was held in awe during the ages due to its physical appearance and properties. The roots of mandrake resemble a human form; Pythagoras called mandrake the "manlike plant." The resemblance of the mandrake root to a human form can be seen in the *Hortus Sanitatis* prints of Johannes de Cuba.

Mandrake's use is probably recorded for the first time in Genesis 30:14-16, which dates back 4000 B.C. In this passage from Genesis, Rachel agrees to let Leah sleep with Jacob one night in exchange for some mandrake plants. Scholars think that Rachel wanted the plant because of its aphrodisiac and fertility properties. Assyrian clay tablets dated 800 B.C. also described the curious properties of the plant.

In the first century A.D., Joseph Flavus wrote the following: "The valley which encloses the north side of the city is called Baara and produces marvelous root of the same name. It is flaming red in color and in the evening emits rays. It is difficult to pull out, for it withdraws when approached and will stay still only when urine or the menstrual blood of women is poured over it. Even then, to touch it is certain death, unless a man carry the whole root away in his hand. But a man may obtain it without danger after another fashion, namely thus: He digs all round it so that only a tiny remnant of the root remains out of sight. He then ties a dog to it and when the dog tries to run after him it tear the root, falling dead on the spot instead of him. Once he has it, the man is in no further danger. People go to all this trouble to obtain it because it possesses the following property. Demons-that is to say the evil spirits of wicked men, which enter into the living and kill them if they are not given speedy aid-are driven out by this plant as soon as it is so much as brought near the sufferer."

In Pliny's time mandrake root was given to patients to chew before operations such as amputations. Patients often preferred the risk of its causing death to the pain that had to be endured. The juice from the bark of the root in wine was used as a sleep inducer or tranquilizer. The leaves of the herb were infused and applied in various forms to ulcers and inflammations. During the fifteenth and sixteenth centuries the berries were believed to possess the power of striking a man dumb. The Arabs collected them and traded them under such names as Devil's Testicles, Devils' Apple, Apple of the Genie and Apple of the Fool. The berries are considered in the Mediterranean region as a delicacy today.

Giambattista Porta wrote about mandragora in his *Phytognomonica*, published in 1588 A.D.: "When you would use it, give it to somebody to drink; and whosoever shall taste it, after a deep sleep will be distracted and for a day shall rave: but after some sleep will return to his senses again, without any harm: and it is very pleasant to behold. Pray make trial."

Mandrake was believed to grow by the gallows. The English romance writer William Harrison Ainsworth embodied these beliefs in the following ballad:

> *At the foot of the gibbet the mandrake springs,*
> *Just where the creaking carcase swings;*
> *Some have thought it engendered*
> *From the fat that drops from the bones of the dead;*
> *Some have thought it a human thing,*
> *But this is a vain imagining.*
> *And whether the mandrake be create*
> *Flesh with the flower incorporate,*
> *I know knot; yet, it from the earth 'tis rent,*
> *Shrieks and groans from the root are sent;...*
> *Whoso gathered the mandrake shall surely die;*
> *Blood for blood is his destiny.*
> *Some who have plucked it have died with groans*
> *Like to the mandrake expiring moans;*

> *Some have died raving, and some beside*
> *With penitent prayers - but all have died.*
> *Jesu! Save us by night and by day*
> *From the terrible death of mandragora!*

Carum petroselinum (Umbelliferae)

This is the Parsley all of us use in our daily cuisine. It has been known to chief master cooks of old times. One reason it is connected to European witchcraft is the Middle Age superstition that the plant was one of Devil's most favorite plants, as discussed below. Another reason might be that it could have been mistaken for the spotted or water hemlock and therefore incorrectly described in old manuscripts. It is sometimes listed as *Apium petroselinum*, *Petroselinum sativum*, *P. crispum* or *P. hortense*.

A third reason is that the plant was associated with death of the Neman King Lycurgus' son Opheltes. The nurse of the infant son of King Lycurgus left the baby unattended while she gave directions to some soldiers. During this time the boy was bitten by a snake. One of the soldiers, the seer Amphiarus, interpreted the death of the child as a bad omen. He foresaw his own death. The soldier gave Opheltes the surname Archemorus, which meant "first to die". From the blood of Opheltes sprang the first parsley plants.

The historian Plutarch recorded an incident when a group of soldiers on their way to battle, fled in panic because they saw a mule with a backload of parsley. The old Greeks strew the plant on the bodies of the dead, and therefore parsley was included in necromantic practices.

Some of the Parsley species have a plain leaf and others a curled. The Greek philosopher Theophrastus described both kinds in his *Enquiry into plants* written about 300 B.C. The curled sort is mostly grown today. It was known to Pliny who sprinkled Parsley seed in his fish ponds to cure sick fish.

The specific name *petroselinum* is derived from the Greek word *petros*, meaning a stone or rock. The name refers to the habitat of the plant, which grows among rocks and stones in the wild. The Greeks bestowed a garland of dried-parsley on the victor of the Isthmian games.

In a book *Le Menagier de Paris* written by a wealthy and elderly Parisian bourgeois for his young wife and published around 1393 A.D. we read: "take parsley and fry it in butter, then pour boiling water on to it and boil it and add salt and serve your sops." It was used in nearly every mediaeval dish that required herbs.

During the Mediaeval period it was believed that once Parsley seed had been sown, the plant will go to the Devil and come back seven (some sources say nine) times before it came up above the ground. The Devil liked it so much that he always kept a little of it. This superstition might be a result of the slow germination of Parsley seeds. Parsley was never to be transplanted because it might bring bad luck to the household.

Another story coming from this period is related to the belief that Parsley seeds cure man's baldness. A vanity so great as to require that a man get up after midnight and sprinkle Parsley seeds on his head. A more "practical" use of the plant was in preventing oneself from getting drunk. If the seeds were taken before drinking alcohol it would "helpth men that have weyke braynes to beare drinks better". This remedy was used by the Romans.

In the sixteenth and seventeenth centuries, the leaves and seeds of parsley were prescribed in various forms to cure different diseases. The leaves of parsley were applied to women's breasts "that are hard through the curding of their milk..." The leaves were also used for curing "contusions, swelled breasts, and enlarged glands." It is possible that the plant was known to the midwife. In modern use, 3-10 drops of parsley seed oil will promote the menstrual flow and ease menstrual pain. Culpeper also wrote that it helped "to provoke urine and the courses, to break wind, both in the stomach and bowels."

Mars

Mars governs Aries (March 21 - April 20). All parts of the head and carotid arteries are under the dominion of this planet.

Euphorbia lathyris (Euphorbiaceae)

This plant is the Caper Spurge. In the Mediaeval Ages the fruits were used for extraction of a very poisonous oil known as the "Oil of Euphorbia." It produces violent purgative effects. Some people in France still use Caper Spurge seeds (about 10-15 seeds) for their laxative action. The mediaeval herbalists recommended that the leaves be well chopped and taken with wine. It was a cure for "choler" and "melancholia". The plant was known to beggars who applied the juice on their skin to raise blisters and in this way excited pity.

The herb belongs to the large Euphorbia genus. The plants are annual or perennial herbs, shrubs and trees, native to the temperate and tropical regions of the world. Their major characteristic is the milky and poisonous juice or sap and that is why they are collectively called Milkwort. Pliny writes that the name Euphorbia commemorates the physician of King Juba II of Mauritania, Euphorbus, who used the juices of these plants in medicine for the first time.

The Caper Spurge is a native to Europe but is also found in the United States. The American native species is the *E. corollata*, called White Purslane. The Caper Spurge is a glabrous annual up to 1 m tall. The leaves are mainly opposite. Its fruits are three sided and hairless, and 8-20 mm long.

Sun

The Sun governs Leo (July 24 - August 23). It influences vitality, oxygen, brain, heart, pituitary gland, and spinal chord.

Paeonia officinalis (**Paeoniaceae**)

Peony is one of the plants that researchers are not sure if it was included in the witches' pharmacopoeia. This herb is believed to be described by the name *Marmaritis*. The plant was listed by Weyer. Peony is mentioned by Pliny in his *Natural History*. According to him, the plant is found growing among the marble quarries of Arabia on the side of Persia. The name *Marmaritis* derives from *marmor*, marble. He was of the opinion that the Magi used the plant to summon deities.

Peony was valued by the ancient Greeks. Its name Paeonia was derived from Paeon. He was the first physician to attended the Gods on Olympus. According to the Greek poet Homer, Paeon healed the wounds of Ares and Hades. Paeonia was also one of the names of Minerva, the healing goddess.

Peony belongs to the family Ranunculaceae, genus Paeonideae. The genus is rather different from the other genera and is treated as a distinct family, the Paeoniaceae. *Paeonia officinalis* and *Paeonia corralina* are very beautiful garden flowers and the pride of every gardener. They are extremely valuable to bees and other pollen collecting insects. Charles Darwin wrote in his book *Effects of cross and self fertilization in the Vegetable Kingdom* (1987) that 3,654,000 pollen grains were counted in a single peony flower.

Paeonia lactiflora, P. suffruticosa and *P. veitchii* are found in Asia and are officially listed in the Chinese Pharmacopoeia. The roots of *Paeonia* are used in traditional Chinese medicine as analgesic, hemostyptic, and bacteriostatic agents. Their major constituent is paeoniflorin, a glucoside of a monoterpene.

The roots of *Paeonia officinalis* were used in Mediaeval Europe. According to Culpeper they "had more virtues than the seed." The root or the seed crushed to a powder and then given in wine were prescribed for "cleansing the womb after childbirth and easing the mother." The black seed was recommended for nightmares and melancholy. The fact that the plant was known to the midwife speaks in favor of the hypothesis that Paeony might have been used in the preparation of the witches' ointment.

In Sussex, England, there was a tradition, according to which, mothers put necklaces of beads made from Peony roots around their children's necks. These necklaces prevented convulsions in the children during the night and were helpful during the process of teething.

Moon

Moon rules Cancer (June 22-July23). It governs fluidic and lymphatic systems, breast, stomach, esophagus, thymus, and memory.

Nymphea alba (**Nymphaeaceae**)

Water Lily was listed in the recipe of Girolamo Cardano. The white Water Lily has large and thick leaves, which float on the water. The flower is snow white. The yellow Water Lily (*Nuphar luteum*) besides the difference in color, has also differences in flower structure compared to the white Water Lily.

The roots of the plant are used to reduce excitement. Culpeper's comments on the use of the roots is very informative: "The roots...will restrain all fluxes, running of the reins and the passing away of seed when one is asleep. Its frequent use extinguishes venerous actions." Decoction of the root may be injected into the vagina to stop leucorrhea. It has also stringent action. The last two properties might have made the plant very useful to the midwife. Oil made from the flowers was used for skin tumors and sores.

No planet assigned to the following plants

Acorus calamus (**Aracea**)

A. calamus is mentioned in Mediaeval books as *acorum*; however its common name is Sweet Flag. Its other names are Calamus Root, Myrtle or Sweet Sedge. The specific name of the plant, *calamus*, is derived from the Greek word *kalamos* or the Sanskrit *kalamas*. Both words mean reed and refer to the use of the glossy leaves of the Sweet Flag for thatching or for floor covers in old times. The generic name, *Acorus*, is derived from the Greek word for eye pupil, *kore*. The ancient Greeks used the plant to treat eye problems.

The Sweet Flag is native to parts of Asia and North and Central America. Nowadays it could be found all over the world. It has been naturalized in the British Isles and most of northern Europe since the beginning of the sixteenth century.

A. calamus is a herbaceous aquatic perennial. Its leaves are sword shaped and up to 1 m long. Its flowers are very small and densely packed on a short branch called spadix. The plant could be found near marshes and swamps, and in the shallow water of rivers and ponds.

Medicinally, the plant has been used for stomach complaints and coughs in Europe, Asia, India and the Arabian countries. It is used very successfully for any problems in the gastro-intestinal system. There are two ways of its preparation. The roots should be washed and cleaned well and then squashed. The juice can be taken for the above complaints. The tea from Acorum roots is prepared only with cold water. The dried roots are ground into powder. One teaspoonful is put into a quarter of a litter of cold water, which is left overnight at room temperature. On the other day the tea should be warmed up. Cheesecloth is used to strain the preparation.

The Acorum roots contain about 4.8% etheric oil. It is yellow-brownish liquid with a very particular smell. The Indians of northern Canada extracted the oil from the roots. Taken internally it induced hallucinations. It is one of the reasons it was included in the witches' ointment.

The root oil contains also ascorbic acid, some terpenes and the alakloid calamine. The oil from the fresh green part smells of tangerine. The major constituent responsible for this characteristic is b-asarone. This compound is similar in structure to safrole. Safrole, a constituent of sassafras (*Sassafras albidum*), as well as b-asarone are used in perfume and soap production. Asarone is also added to gin and beer for flavor. Experimental rats fed with high doses of calamus developed mesenchymal tumors of the small intestine. Such effects in man have not been reported and the plant is used medicinally with great success. Sweet flag roots are very effective against moths.

Daphne laureola, D. mezereum and *D. gnidium* (Thymelaeceae)

As mentioned earlier, Apulieus, in *The Golden Ass* wrote that the witch Pamphile would turn herself into a bird after using a concoction made of laurel and dill dissolved in water. The name Dwarf Laurel is used for *Daphne mezereum,* while the Spurge Laurel is *Daphne laureola.*

The Daphnes consist of about 40 evergreen or deciduous species. They are native to Europe including the Alpine regions. In the Greek mythology, Daphne was the daughter of the river god.

In the Middle Ages *Daphne mezereum* was the species most often used for medicinal purposes. According to Culpeper "a decocotion made of a dram of the bark of the root in three pints of water, till one pint is wasted, and this quantity taken in the course of the day, for a considerable time together, has been found very efficacious in resolving and dispersing venereal swellings and excrescencies."

The Dwarf Laurel was known to be poisonous. Culpeper warned that if the bark of the root was to be used, it required "caution in the administration, and must only be given to people of robust constitutions." Despite of this fact, the Laurel was used as much as 30 berries by the Russian peasantry as a body purge, while the French thought 15 berries were the fatal dose. In Germany a tincture of Laurel berries was prescribed for neuralgias.

✍ **More botanical notes:**

Chapter 7
OINTMENT PREPARATION

> *"Stir, stir about, whilst I begin the charm,*
> *Black spirits and white, red spirits and gray,*
> *Mingle, mingle, mingle, you that mingle may,*
> *Round, around, around about, about!"*
>
> Middleton, *The Witch*

Recipes recorded in witches' confessions during trials were not exact. The Inquisitors were not interested in such details. The recipes of the ointment probably varied from one region to the other throughout Europe. Depending on the preparer's experience and regional tradition variation could occur but the basic ingredients were universal. This assumption is based on similarity between old herbal recipes from geographically distant parts of Europe. For example, there is similarity in the use of plants in the Swiss mountainous regions and the Balkan Peninsula. The recipes were passed from one man to another. With the increase in Inquisitorial prosecutions and victims, fewer people practiced the "flying" to the Sabbat by means of the ointment and the recipes remained in oblivion.

A witches' ointment recipe was discovered by Siegbert Ferckel who published consequently his experiences with the unguent in the German magazine *Kosmos*. The author admitted that the formulation of the recipe was very vague but he still experimented with it. He did not list the particular ingredients but from what follows below it could be concluded that the major plant ingredients were the ones already discussed previously.

Mr. Ferckel anointed only the area on his chest above his heart. Since he did not experience anything after 45 minutes, he applied the whole ointment all over his chest. Five minutes past and he felt that his heart started beating very fast. He looked at himself in the mirror and got scared because his pupils were wide open and his lips were blue. His limbs became numb and he lost control of his body. The whole room was spinning around. The ceiling was undulated like giant waves. He started seeing horrible faces peeking from around the window frames, which stared at him. There was some kind of fog and sounds as if coming from a clay pipe. He wrote that his perception of time changed and every minute was like an eternity.

The effects of the ointment prepared by Mr. Ferckel are very similar to the already described effects of henbane, mandragora, and some of the other plants discussed previously.

I obtained recollections about the usage of a similar concoction in the form of tea from a herbalist from the Stakevtsi region in Stara Planina. The ingredients were as the ones mentioned above. The plants for the witches' ointment have been used in herbal medicine for centuries to treat different diseases. Ways of harvesting and storage are as follow.

Harvesting

Conium maculatum is harvested during July and August by cutting the upper parts (*herba Conii maculati*) of the plant. **Children in any way should not collect the plant because it is poisonous.** The cuttings are to be sun dried or dried in a special drier and stored in dry facilities.

Almost all parts of *Atropa belladonna* could be used for medicinal purposes. The roots (*radix Atropae belladonnae*), the leaves (*folia Atropae belladonnae*), and stalks (*herba Atropae belladonnae*) contain the alkaloid atropine. Only the roots of plants that are 2-3 years old should be taken out of the ground in the Fall. They should be washed well and cut in pieces about 8-10 cm. The leaves are collected with their petioles (about 2 cm). Then they are dried.

Leaves of the black henbane (*folia Hyosciami nigri*) are usually collected for medicinal applications. It is advisable to collect the well grown leaves at the end of the summer. The petioles should be cut about 2 -3 cm from the leaves. The harvested leaves should be dried 5-6 hours in the sun and then the drying should be continued with the leaves being in the shade.

Leaves of the Thornapple (*folia Daturae stramonii*) are collected in July or August when the plant is flowering. They should be dried in the shadow, in a well ventilated place.

Roots of the Sweet Flag can be used unpeeled (*rhizoma calami naturalis*) or peeled (*rhizoma calami mund.*). They should be collected in the Fall when the water level has decreased. They are taken out of the mud, washed, cut in 8-10 cm pieces and dried.

Purple Foxglove leaves (*folia Digitalis purpuraea*) should be collected in July or early August. They must be dried only in the shadow.

All other plants discussed in the previous chapter could be collected in the same way. The plants are poisonous. **Children must avoid any contact with them.**

Storage of Herbs

All herbs must be dried and stored in well ventilated storage rooms if gathered in large quantities. Herbs as a rule are stored in dry glass jars or cardboard boxes. Avoid storing dried plants in plastic or metal containers. Dried plants must not be exposed to sunlight. If you are using glass jars it is advisable to wrap them up with aluminum foil or paper.

Ointment Preparation

Herbal ointments are usually prepared in the following way.

> R_x
> - A half of kilogram of pork lard is heated in a frying pan until sizzling.
> - The herbs (four handfuls) are added and fried by stirring about one minute.
> - The pan is taken off the stove, covered with a lid and left overnight. During this time all the alkaloids and other substances are extracted from the plants.
> - On the next day, the preparation is heated up until it becomes liquid.
> - Then it is strained through cheesecloth and poured in small glass or porcelain containers. It is preferable to store the ointment in a cool place.

The author Jong gives a "Traditional English" recipe in his book *Witches*. Some of the ingredients were not available to the common practitioner of the Art during the Mediaeval times and even nowadays. Moreover, such a psychedelic concentrated preparation is nothing else but a pure poison.

R_x
- 30 grams betel
- 50 grams extract of opium
- 6 grams cinquefoil
- 15 grams henbane
- 15 grams belladonna
- 3 grams annamthol
- 15 grams hemlock
- 250 grams cannabis
- 5 grams cathreindin

Blend with oil of your choice.

A "Modern American" recipe recommends the ingredients given below. I can not give recommendations for the brand of perfume to be used because I believe that it depends on your preferences. However, do not buy a cheap fragrance. After all, if the recipe is not potent your social status might at least depend on the qualities of the perfume.

R_x
- ½ tsp. Wolfbane juice
- ½ belladonna
- 1 tsp. vegetable oil
- 1 jar cream
- 3 drops liquid detergent

Mix with perfume.

The content of the alkaloids in the plants used for the witches' ointment very from one geographical region to another and from one season to another. It is not advisable to give an exact recipe for this preparation. It might be achieved through experimentation but the use of the ointment is very dangerous. Any experimentation with these plants is life threatening.

Chapter 8

MECHANISMS OF THE OINTMENT ACTION

The role of the witches' ointment in the diabolical craft has been debated by theological and academic researchers through the centuries. Some authors in the Middle Ages claimed that the ointment had absolutely no effects on the user without the interference of the Devil. Others considered the ointment as a potent hallucinogenic causing all the experiences of the witches, yet still a convenient tool of the Devil.

In his academic dissertation presented in November 19, 1698 A.D. at the University of Rostock (Germany), Johann Klein discussed the use of ointments in flying and beast transformations. He wrote that those "who really think themselves converted into beasts ...... fall into deep sleep when they anoint themselves, and when they awake believe that they have been changed to wolves..." He analyzed the power of the ointments and concluded that the whole process is the work of the Devil. The means employed, i.e. the ointment, had no power by themselves and the Devil made his servants use them to conceal his own agency.

Adam Tanner (1629 A.D.) supported the theory of delusions. He wrote about a woman who had promised a man to come to his chamber that night. The man waited for her and because she did not keep her promise, he went to her house. He found the woman lying insensible and naked in her own room with another woman, also naked and anointed. After the woman recovered from her "sleep", she claimed to have been with her lover in his room. Tanner was convinced that the woman's stories were the result of hallucinations induced by the ointment.

The belief in the power of witches grew to such an extent that Pierre Node from Paris (1578 A.D.) blamed all the misfortunes of France upon the practitioners of the diabolic art. Among the activities they employed, according to the author, were delusions and hallucinations.

Francesco Maria Guaccio of the Order of St. Ambrosius at Nemus (1608 A.D.) wrote that the followers of Luther (Devil) hold that the witch only went to the Sabbat through diabolic illusion. They did that by anointing themselves with unguents. The truth, according to him, was that sometimes they were transported by demons.

During the Mediaeval period, some physicians, scientists, theologians and even inquisitors considered the ointment to be a narcotic drug. The reported experiences of the witches were said to be hallucinations and dreams that had nothing to do with real flights to the Sabbat. The inquisitor Alonso de Salazar y Frias, who presided as a judge at the 1610 A.D. trials in towns along the banks of the River Ezcurra (Bask province) cross-examined witches and witnesses to prove that the flights to the Sabbat in the witches' confessions were not real.

Some mediaeval scientists were interested to learn why witches reported stories of flights in the air after the use of the ointment. As described earlier in this book, the Mediaeval author Gassendi performed an experiment with a narcotic concoction prepared according to a recipe given to him by a sorcerer. He applied the potion to several villagers living in the Basses Alps. He told them that they were going to the Sabbat. The villagers fell into a deep sleep. After they regained consciousness, they related their experiences of flights to the Sabbat. Another scientist, Malebranche, also firmly believed in the narcotic effects of the ointment. He analyzed the psychological state of its users after they anointed themselves. Malebranche concluded that they became vulnerable to suggestions, beliefs and ideas, which were distorted and amplified after the application of the ointment.

The physician Weyer discussed the use of plants and their effects in several chapters of his book. His Spanish colleague Laguna experimented with the ointment on a neurotic woman, as explained previously. The conclusions from his experiments were that the witches claims of transportation through the air were "a dream caused by cold drinks and unguents." Weyer and Laguna were supporters of the narcotic action hypothesis. Laguna, true to his time, wrote that "the Devil can not work except through natural causes" and his knowledge of such ointments allowed him to manipulate the minds of his servants.

In 1921, Professor A.J. Clark wrote a comment entitled "Flying ointments" appenidixed in Margaret Murray's book *The witch cult in Western Europe*. He analyzed briefly the poisonous plants and concluded that the drugs might affect the action of the heart and thus, produce the sensation of flying.

I propose that alkaloids contained in plants used by the witches of Mediaeval Europe cause death when taken orally in quantities exceeding a certain threshold of toxicity. If they are taken via other routes in doses lower than the lethal level they cause hallucinogenic effects. People in ancient times discovered that slow penetration of a low dose of these alkaloids might cause exhilaration and pleasant mental experiences. A way to administer these compounds into the body was the application of ointments.

According to the written accounts from witch trials the ointment was applied onto the skin of different parts of the body or through mucosal route by use of the broomstick, which was anointed with it. The latter application is discussed in the next chapter. In modern, as well as in ancient medicine, the advantage of drug administration via an ointment is due to the mechanical protection of the skin by the vehicle. The skin is lubricated and softened, and the medication has easier access into the body. Ointments do not permit drainage or evaporation of the compounds from the skin, and thus allowing **constant but slow availability** of the administered drug. Ointments hold the drug(s) tightly and allow too little to be released.

Studies indicate that drugs penetrate the skin predominantly by passing through a lipid-like barrier in the epidermal layer of the skin. The dermis has the characteristics of a highly porous membrane. The main route of drugs through the skin has been debated by scientists for some time. Some researchers argued that drugs penetrate the skin easily through the hair follicles, sweat glands and sebaceous glands. It was shown that this route is not better than the skin itself. In fact, regions of the skin devoid of hair follicles, i.e. hairless, were penetrated more rapidly than regions covered by hair. Application of an ointment in hairy areas might cause *folliculitis* (inflammation of the hair follicle) due to the penetration of the ointment to the base of the follicle. Dissolving the drug in a fatty carrier, as shown by numerous experiments enhances absorption through the skin.

The vehicle in an ointment is of almost no value (besides skin protection from dryness) without the drug. In most cases the "flying ointment" included extracts from Aconite (*Aconitum* spp.), Deadly Nightshade (*Atropa belladonna*), Jimson Weed (*Datura stramonium*) or Black Henbane (*Hyoscyamus niger*). Their active constituents are aconitine, hyoscyamine, atropine and scopolamine.

The secret in the ointment's preparation is based on the use of two poisons, which antagonize each other's action. Each of them is deadly but when used together they mutually reduce their poisonous effect, i.e. the action of aconitine and atropine is antagonistic. For example, if a patient has been poisoned by Aconite consumption, one of the remedies is treatment with atropine at 2 milligrams introduced subcutaneously and repeated as needed. Atropine is an effective antidote used in different cases. Antidote is a therapeutic substance used to counteract the toxic action(s) of a specific xenobiotic. For example, atropine in combination with some other compounds, is used as an antidote against poisoning with organophosphate nerve gas agents, which are a serious threat on the battlefield.

The inclusion of both atropine and aconitine in an ointment makes the preparation harmless to a certain extent. A slight predominance of one of them will bring the necessary exhilarating effects. Which alkaloid should exceed the other and how much one should add from the other alkaloid sources, depends on the recipe and the person preparing it.

Today, the progress in neurobiology research makes it possible to analyze the mechanism of action of the witches' ointment. The analysis of the effects of plant alkaloids on the nervous system requires a short and simplified description of the way nervous signals are transmitted.

The nervous system has two types of cells called nerve cells or neurons and glial cells (or glia). The human brain contains about 1,000,000,000,000 neurons. A neuron consists of a central region, termed cell body that has two types of projections. The first type is represented by several **dendrites** in a neuron, which receive the information from other cells. The neuron transmits information to neighboring cells by means of the second type of projection called **axon**. The axon is connected to dendrites and cell bodies of other cells. The point of contact is known as a **synapse**.

A signal from a neuron to another neuron or effector organ is transmitted via the so-called chemical transmitters. These are substances, which are synthesized in the neurons, released from them at the synapses and bound to receptor neurons or organs. When this substance is acetylcholine the transmission is called cholinergic. When the transmitter is adrenaline or dopamine, the transmission is called adrenergic or dopaminergic, correspondingly.

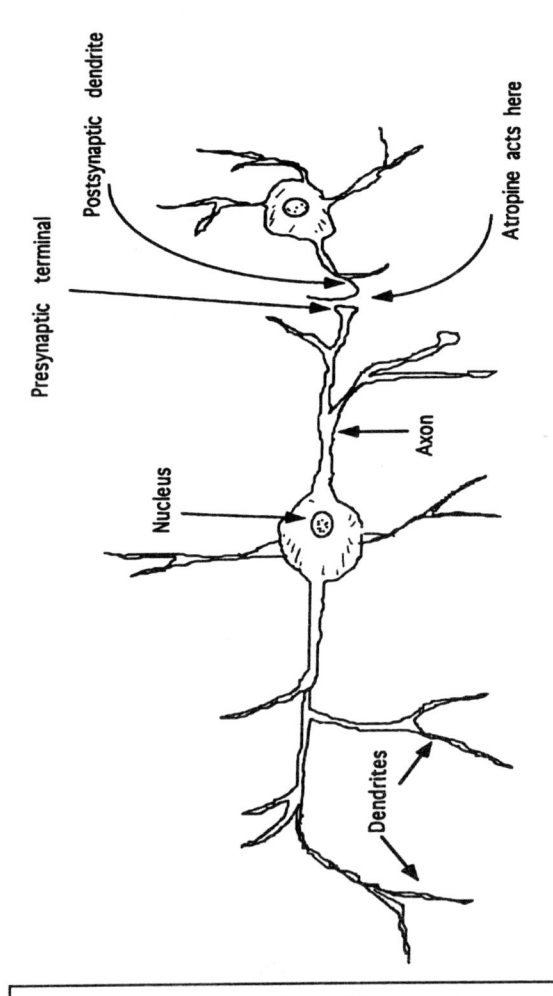

Schematic presentation of interaction between neuronal cells through a synapse.

Problems in nerve signal transmission leads to neuropathological conditions as schizophrenia. Although schizophrenia affects one in every 100 individuals and is a much investigated clinical field, medical researchers still have no universally accepted definition. The disease is accompanied by delusions, eccentric or violent behavior, hallucinations, and social inadequacy. The drugs used in such cases are called "psychotropic" drugs. They are intended to have a curative effect on the patient.

In contrast, drugs that have been tested on subjects with adequate psychological balance to study intoxication similar to psychosis are called "psychotomimetics." This group of drugs is sometimes described by various other names. The term "hallucinogen" is used implying a general property of hallucination induction by the drugs, which is not always correct. The word "psychedelic" was coined in the sixties of this century and is related to the popular then fashion of using substances for altering the states of mind consciousness.

The alkaloids found in the plants used for the witches' ointment have anticholinergic effects. They act primarily on the cholinergic synapses. Atropine and scopolamine, due to their structural similarity to acetylcholine, (see Figure on the next page) block its action. Various scientific experiments have been performed on men as well as on animals to study the action of psychedelic drugs, including the alkaloids found in the witches' ointment.

Perception in the human brain depends on groups of neurons, termed neuronal ensembles, rather than on individual neurons. Each neuron has a separation of electrical charge across its membrane. Changes in the electrical activity of a neuronal ensemble can be measured and recorded by **electroencephalogram** (EEG). In this non-invasive procedure, numerous electrodes are placed on the scalp of the patient. The electrical activity of the brain can be recorded while the subject is sleeping or sitting relaxed.

Acetylcholine

R = H,H; *Atropine*
R = -O-; *Scopolamine*

Some studies attempted to correlate the electroencephalographic with the behavioral effect of some psychotomimetic drugs, including atropine. Hallucinations, delusions and tremors were recorded in the studied subjects due to the administration of the drug Ditran, which is structurally related to atropine. These experiences were accompanied by desynchronization of the EEG pattern. In contrast, such desynchronization was not recorded after atropine administration. The study showed that symptoms such as euphoria, relaxation, and drowsiness are associated with synchronization of the encephalographic pattern.

To further investigate the processes connected to the effect of these drugs, scientists performed experiments on cats. After atropine treatment the cats showed hyperactivity, disturbance (crying and whining) and defensive behavior upon approach. Atropine had a marked activity on the hippocampus occasionally producing seizures. The hippocampus is a part of the limbic system in the brain and is involved in memory storage. The limbic system is thought to take part in emotions because damage to the area affects emotional expression.

Most antipsychotic drugs act on serotonin receptors. These receptors are also the site of action of lysergic acid diethylamide (LSD) and other psychedelic hallucinogens. Other studies with cats showed that atropine had effects similar to these observed with LSD and mescaline on the hippocampus activities.

The therapeutic administration of drugs that act on adrenoreceptors has been accompanied, although in a low incidence, by various side effects. These include vivid dreams, visual, auditory and tactile hallucinations, disorientation and paranoid delusions. Such cases suggest that psychedelic drugs do exert central effects on the nervous system in man and can be compared to the alkaloid action from plants used in the witches' concoctions.

The ointment was also used by midwives during their assistance in abortions and childbirths. They discovered that the ointment induced labor when applied to the vagina. The vaginal wall consists of three layers, namely the epithelial layer, the muscular coat, and the tunica adventitia. The epithelial layer contains three different types of epithelia, which contact each other in a very small area. The epithelium is noncornified in contrast to the skin and therefore penetrable. The vagina is enveloped by a dense net of arteries supplying blood to it and veins ensuring proper drainage of blood from the vagina.

Absorption from the vaginal walls depends on the size and chemical nature of the compound. The pioneer student of the type of compounds that are absorbed by the vaginal walls, was the American scientist David Macht. He worked at the John Hopkins Medical School early in this century. Macht concentrated his efforts on this particular research because the prevalent opinion among his colleagues was that drugs applied to the vagina exert only local effect and are not absorbed by the system.

At the beginning of the nineteenth century physicians were still uncertain about knowledge that had been used by practitioners of witchcraft earlier. An accused "serial" killer in Italy from this time, however, had no doubts about the permeability of vaginal walls. He murdered his first wife by somehow administering arsenic in her vagina. Married a second time, he repeated the same procedure but this time was discovered. Reports of deaths from vaginal douches suggested the ability of the vagina to absorb chemicals.

Macht performed experiments on cats and dogs. The vaginal mucosa of dogs is histologically similar to the human vagina. He studied the absorption of many chemicals by the vagina and their passage to the blood stream. In 1927, Robinson performed experiments on cats and dogs with the objective to test if and what substances are absorbed by the vaginal walls. He showed that the walls of the vagina rapidly absorb the alkaloids strychnine and pilocarpine. Atropine in the form of sulfate salt was easily absorbed and caused an increase in blood pressure. Fats are absorbed from the vaginal lumen. Olive oil was not absorbed by the vagina walls of experimental animals.

Today, atropine has been shown to cross the placenta and affect the fetus. Therefore, too strong preparation of the ointment could have caused undesired outcomes during the midwife procedures. In most cases such failures brought death to the midwives due to witchcraft accusations.

The using of the ointment during delivery may be produced its hallucinatory effects on the patients. The experiments above suggest that there might be truth behind the witches' statements about anointing the broom as will be described further in this book.

The action of the witches' ointment may not be such a mystery today. The ointment was probably the last remnant of the paraphernalia of magicians, shamans and oracles on the European continent. It was a parting cry to an ancient art of mind travel into the realm of the unknown.

Spiritual journeys of people on the European continent, called "benandanti", were reported by Carlo Ginzburg. The benandanti were people born with the caul and initiated into a special sect. These people traveled and attended their meetings "in spirit". While their bodies remained in bed during the night, their spirits traveled. Their aim was to fight against destructive witches at certain times of the year. The outcome of these spiritual battles would determine the fate of the coming harvest. The benandanti were defenders of fertility against the witches causing bad weather and sterility in crops and domestic animals.

The members of the benandanti sect never used ointments. They spoke of deep sleeps and lethargies. Only in two later benandanti trials (1626 A.D.), when the Inquisition started suspecting the sect of the practice of Diabolical crafts, did the accused mention greasing themselves with lamp oil. Torture was used, however, during the interrogations and the confessions might have not been truthful.

Soul travel is also characteristic of women who contacted the *samodivas* in the Balkans. Nothing points to the use of an ointment, although the use of herbs has been recorded. During my personal training with herbalists in the Western Balkans (Stara Planina) it was always pointed out that the proportions of different herbs gave the power in a preparation. It could be speculated that the ointment technique of witches for soul travel evolved from the self-hypnotic ways of the benandanti. It was more easily achieved and available to everyone without a special gift.

During the night travels, witches had their familiars or animal forms they adopted. These were similar but not exactly what the "nagual" would be to the Chiapa Indians. The nagual is the "animal-companion", "animal-soul" of the Chiapa sorcerer. The nagual represents the individual in the spiritual realm. The way to this realm starts through the use of herbs and later through mind techniques supervised by a master sorcerer. Was then, the witches' ointment an easier way to go out of the real world than the seeking of a spiritual guide?

The Inquisitorial prosecutions in Europe eradicated the knowledge and the practice of the ointment preparation. The anointing ritual remained in oblivion and was revived only during this century. The real ointment however, has not been very popular among practitioners of Neo-Pagan rituals because of its deadly nature if prepared incorrectly. As in every art, a real Master is always needed but never easy to find.

Chapter 9

FLYING ON A BROOM

"For certain rituals... a phallic wand is used."

Janet & Stewart Farrar, *The wicthes' way*

L iving in our imagination since childhood is the image of a witch flying on her broom. Fairy tale books have fascinating pictures of old and evil witches riding their brooms and occasionally haunting the young listener or reader's dreams. The witch is always inseparable from her broomstick. One could assume that this image is universal for both the Old and New Continents.

The common belief that witches rode on the broomstick to the places of their gatherings was reflected in art from this time. The earliest picture of a witch riding on her broom is in the cathedral at Schleswig in Germany thought to be drawn in the 1280s A.D. In most of the Middle Age prints witches are depicted completely naked on their means of transportation.

The broomstick was used not only for transportation but also as a means to conceal the woman's absence during the night. According to the confessions of Isobel Gowdie at Aildearn, in Nairn, in 1662 A.D., she and her accomplices would place a broom in the bed, beside their husbands, which promptly took the appearance of a woman. In this case, the vehicles to the Sabbat were horses, which the women made of "a straw or a bean-stalk." Isobel's confessions were extracted under torture and as pointed out by Prof. Cohn, she drew on local fairy folklore to satisfy her interrogators.

Instead of a broom, in Bulgarian folklore, and more particularly in the western parts of Stara Planina, a representative of the fairy world, called *krosnojhazlitsa* would carry a yarn beam. The name is made up from *krosno*, which means yarn beam and *jhaz*, water pool. The *krosnojhazlitsi* (plural) are women who danced by the rivers and caused harm to anyone who dared approach their meeting place.

In his book *The roots of witchcraft*, Harrison suggested that the verb "ride" is a euphemism of the word for "sexual congress." He further speculated that the expression "between the witches' legs" is also a euphemism to be understood not between but "within." According to Harrison, the broomstick is nothing but a mediaeval equivalent of the ancient ritual object called *olisbos* or as the Classical writers called it *penis coriaceus*. This is the boiled and moulded leather that women bore in the Bacchic procession and the artificial penis that the Devil has been reported to wear during the Sabbat gatherings.

The broomstick was heavily coated with the witches' ointment. As Harrison commented, such a broomstick "placed against the absorbent membrane within the *labia majora*, the delirifacient would soon penetrate the linings of the vaginal and urethral tracts..." This hypothesis is highly possible considering the records of witch trials pertaining to broom sticks and other "short sticks", and the anatomy of the vagina discussed previously. The broomstick or other short sticks were a means of applying the "flying" ointment to a particular permeable port of the female body.[*] The idea of riding the broom in reality is closely connected to its use as a means of ointment application.

The broomstick is closely connected with the magic wand or staff of sorcerers, which was considered equally

---

[*] Faber's book *Modern Witchcraft and Psychoanalysis* would be useful for the reader interested in psychoanalysis of witches and their activities.

serviceable for purposes of equitation. In southern France the sorcerers used the dogwood (*Cornus sanguinea*) for the broom construction.

The brooms or besoms in Europe were made from *Cytisus scoparius* whose common name is the Common Broom. It is a shrub growing from 1-2 to 4 m and flowering in May and June. The plant is found throughout Europe, and also on the Mediterranean islands. The common Broom was valuable in rural economy as a principal winter food for sheep in the mountainous districts of Scotland. In the southern parts of Europe the shrub attains a bigger size and the wood is used for veneering.

Another plant used for broom construction, especially in Italy, was *Ruscus aculeatus*, whose common name is the Butcher's Broom. People used to put the boughs of the plant around bacon and cheese to defend from mice, hence the German name *mauserdorn*. In England, the plant was used to make little brooms or scrubbing brushes for cleaning the kitchen utensils.

Brooms in SouthEastern Europe have always been made of sorghum (*Sorghum bicolor*). In the Middle Ages, bad witches and warlocks in Italy were armed with stalks of sorghum. Their "good" counterparts, the *benandanti*, used bundles of fennel (*Foeniculum vulgare*) as weapons.

When we talk about witches' brooms sometimes the bush witch hazel comes to mind. This is the common name for *Hamamelis virginiana* plant. The witch-plant is native of North America, from Canada to Florida. The early American settlers used its branches as a divining rod in search of underground water sources or gold. It is also possible that the name was transferred from the English "wych hazel" originating from *wican*, to yield. Witch hazel was introduced into Europe in 1736 A.D., and grown in gardens because of its flowers which remain on the shrub very late in the Fall.

The bark of the witch hazel was valued by the native Americans because of its sedative effects. For hundreds of years the oil from Witch Hazel has been believed to cure a variety of bodily problems. It is usually mixed with alcohol and used for rubbing aching parts of the body nowadays. The leaves and the branches of the plant are used in toiletries.

The broom has found a significant place in Barbara Broughel's art. In her series *Requiem* she presents 42 objects that stand as portraits of people convicted or punished for witchcraft in seventeenth-century America. The artist designed brooms and other household implements, which she humanized with clothing to create memorials to the doomed witches. For example, the "portrait" of Elizabeth Kendall, who was convicted in Cambridge, Massachusetts in 1647 for "having familiarity with Satan", is a broomcorn brush with linen collar.

The broom is not the main transportation to the Sabbat. It is only a symbol that has remained in the folklores. It is the ointment that facilitates the travel during the nights.

Chapter 10

NOCTURNAL FLIGHTS

D oes the power of the ointment come from its correct chemical composition or are there any other important factors?

From a pharmacological stand point of view the exact proportions of recipe constituents do matter. The importance of creating the right balance between aconitine and atropine is unquestionable. An overdose of one compound will turn your salve into a strong poison.

However, good herbalist skills still do not guarantee a good flight according to many practitioners. There are special nights during the year when flights are extremely rewarding. Usually a fool moon is a good sign. The ritual should be performed with fellow practitioners under the guidance of a Master or well-experienced herbalist. Never perform it alone for the ointment might have turned more potent with time (due to evaporation and therefore becoming more concentrated). Perspiration accompanies the experiences and if the body is not covered with a woolen blanket it might catch a cold.

The ointment is usually applied by slight massaging on the temples. It is recommended that the ointment be not applied to any mucosal barriers of the body.

Prepare yourself for an indescribable journey. It is a dangerous one, too.[1]

---

[1] The author does not encourage anyone under any circumstances to experiment with these preparations. Such practices are life threatening! Despite the available scientific data most of the discussions are speculative.

GLOSSARY

Alkaloid: a basic nitrogenous secondary compound found in plants.
Alternate (leaves): leaf arrangement when only one leaf is at any one level of the stem.
Analgesic: producing insensibility to pain.
Annual: a plant completing its entire life cycle in one growing season and dying back in the winter.
Aphrodisiac: provocative of or exciting sexual desire.
Astringent: producing contraction of organic tissue, or arrest of a discharge.
Axil: the upper angle that a leaf stalk or petiole makes with the stem from which it grows.
Biennial: a plant which completes its life cycle in two years.
Calyx: a collective term for the sepals of a flower.
Capsule: a type of fruit, which is dry, splits along two or more lines, and has more than one row of seeds.
Cardiotoxic: negatively affecting the proper functioning of the heart (for a substance).
Congenital: existing at or dating from birth.
Cotyledon: the first leaf produced by an embryo of a flowering plant.
Cranial: pertaining to the skull (cranium, Latin).
Deciduous: a tree shedding its leaves annually.
Dilation of pupils: enlargement of the pupils.
Edema: a swelling with abnormal accumulation of fluid in a body tissue.
Ester: the product of a chemical reaction of an alcohol and a carboxylic acid.
Hemolytic: inducing hemolysis.
Hemotoxic: poisonous to the blood.

Hippomanes: a growth found on the forehead of a newborn foal.
Indolent tumor: tumor not causing pain.
Laxative: medicine producing bowel movement and relieving constipation.
Leucorrhea: Vaginal discharge.
Mesenchymal: belonging to the loosely organized mesodermal connective tissue (mesenchyme).
Myotoxic: causing harm to the muscles (for a substance).
Necromantic: magic directed to attain evil purposes.
Neurotoxic: damaging the nervous system (for a substance).
Palmate: radiating from a common point.
Peptide: a molecule consisting of aminoacids linked by a peptide bond (-CO-NH-).
Pinnate: arranged along a central axis.
Perennial: a plant which comes up year after year.
Poultice: soft and moist mass of herbs applied to sores to supply warmth and moisture.
Protein: nitrogenous compounds occurring in all living matter and essential to the diet of animals.
Purgative: purging, cleansing medicine.
Raceme: elongated and slender inflorescence as in grasses.
Spasmolytic: medicine, which relieves spasms or convulsions.
Steroids: compounds that have the steroid nucleus, which is consists of four fused carboxylic rings.
Stupor: partial or complete unconsciousness.
Styptic: a substance that holds bleeding by contracting the tissues or blood vessels.
Tincture: a solution of medicinal substance (as a plant principle) in alcohol.
Umbel: a branched flat-topped cluster of small flowers.

APPENDIX

Notes on chemical formulas used as illustration to the text

The primary objective of this book is to discuss plant and animal ingredients used by European witches to prepare a ritual ointment and the mechanisms of its action. The active ingredients in the ointment are alkaloids. The representations of their molecules can be drawn. Formulas in organic molecules (molecules found in organic/live matter) can be given with a bond-line drawing. In these formulas the chemical bonds are represented by a line, i.e. ———. These formulas are given in the text to illustrate the chemical nature of the compounds and stimulate the interested reader for further studies in this field.

The carbon atom is denoted **C**, the hydrogen atom **H**, and the nitrogen atom **N**. Hydrocarbons are compounds that are composed entirely of carbon and hydrogen atoms. If these hydrocarbons are straight or branched they are known as alkanes. For example, CH_3——CH_2——CH_3. Alkanes can consist of more than three carbon atoms and they can be closed. In such a case they are called cyclic alkanes and they form a ring. In each corner of this ring the carbon atoms may not be written.

If all the atoms in the ring are not alike, the compounds are known as heterocyclic compounds. The heteroatom in the rings of alkaloids is nitrogen, **N**. Alkaloids have also functional groups protruding from the rings.

Abbreviations and measurement units

A.D. : anno domini (Latin) = in the year of our Lord
B.C.: before Christ
cm (centimeter) = 10^{-2} m
kilogram (kg): = 2.205 lb
m (meter) = 0.304 ft
milligram (mg) = 10^{-3} kg

BIBLIOGRAPHY AND RECOMMENDED LITERATURE

1. Anderson, F.J. An illustrated history of the herbals. Columbia, University Press, New York, 1977
2. Baroja, J.C. The world of the witches. The University of Chicago Press, Chicago, 1964
3. Boquet, H. An examen of witches. Allan, E. (translator), London, p. xxxix,1929
4. Buxton, D.A., Greenwood, D.T., Middlemiss, D.N. Central nervous actions of b-adrenoreceptor antagonists. In: Hoffmeister, F., Stille, G. (Eds.) Psychotropic agents. Part I: Antipsychotics and antidepressents. Springer Verlag Berlin Heidelberg, pp 349-367, 1980
5. Byrne, P.F. Witchcraft in Ireland. The Mercier Press, Bridge Street, Cork, 1967
6. Castaneda, C. The teachings of Don Juan: a Yaqui way of knowledge. Washington Square Press, New York, 1968
7. Castaneda, C. Tales of power. A Touchstone Book, New York, 1974
8. Clarke, A.J. Flying ointments. In: Murray, M.A. The witch-cult in Western Europe. Clarendon Press, Oxford, pp 279-280, 1921
9. Cohn, N.R.C. Europe's inner demons: an enquiry inspired by the great witch-hunt. Basic Books, New York, 1975
10. Conklin, G.N. Alkaloids and the witches' Sabbat. American journal of pharmacy and the sciences supporting public health. 30:171-174, 1958
11. Culpeper, N. Culperper's color herbal. Potterton, D. (Ed.). Sterling Publishing Co., Inc., New York, 1983
12. de Givry, G. A pictorial anthology of witchcraft, magic and alchemy. University Books, Chicago & New York, 1958
13. Delrio. Disquitiones magicae, Liber II, qto xvi. (cited in Summers 1971)

14. Dolara, P., Luceri, C., Ghelardini, C., Monserrat, C., Aiolli, S., Luceri, F., Lodovici, M., Menichetti, S., Romanelli, M.N. Analgesic effects of myrrh. Nature, 379:29, 1996
15. Faber, M.D. Modern witchcraft and psychoanalysis. Associated University Press, Cranbury, NJ, 1993
16. Ferckel, S. 'Hexensalbe' und ihre Wirkung. Kosmos, Gesellschaft d. Naturfreunde. 50:414-415, 1954
17. Fletcher, R. The witches' pharmacopoeia. Bulletin of the Johns Hopkins hospital. VII:147-156, 1896
18. Forbes, T.R. The midwife and the witch. Yale University Press, New Haven, 1966
19. Franklyn, J. Death by enchantment. Hamish Hamilton, London, 1971
20. Frazer, Sir J. The new golden bough. A Mentor Book, New York, 1964
21. Freeman, K. Shaman Pharmaceuticals follows an "Eco" approach to new drug development. Genetic Engineering News, May 15:14-15, 1994
22. Freeman, M.B. Herbs for the mediaeval household for cooking, healing and divers uses. The Metropolitan Museum of Art, New York, 1943
23. Friendenwald, H. Andres a Laguna, a pioneer in his views on witchcraft. Bulletin of the history of medicine. 7:1037-1048, 1939
24. Gardner, G.B. Witchcraft today. Rider, London, 1954
25. Ginzburg, C. The night battle. Witchcraft and agrarian cults in the sixteenth and seventeenth centuries. The Johns Hopkins University Press, Baltimore, 1983
26. Gross, H.A., Jones, W.I., Cook, E.L., Boone, C.C. Carcinogenicity of oil of calamus. Proceedings of the American Association for Cancer Research 8:24-27, 1967
27. Haarstad, V.B. Witchcraft: a pharmacological analysis. Bulletin of the Tulane University medical faculty. 24:51-68, 1964
28. Habermehl, G.G. Venomous animals and their toxins. Springer-Verlag, Berlin Heidelberg, 1981
29. Hardin, J.W., Arena J.M. Human poisoning from native and cultivated plants. Duke University Press, North Carolina, 1974

30. Harrison, M. The roots of witchcraft. The Citadel Press, Secaucus, NJ, 1974
31. Hartman, C.G. The permiability of the vaginal mucosa. Annals of the New York Academy of Sciences, 83:318-327, 1959
32. Jacobsen, D. The relative efficacy of antidotes. Clinical Toxicology, 33:705-708, 1995
33. Johnson, A.E. Photosynthesizing toxins from plants and their biological effects. In: Keeler, R.F., Tu, A.T. (Eds.) Handbook of natural toxins vol. 1, Plant and fungal toxins. Marcel Dekker, Inc. New York, pp 345-359, 1983
34. Kandel, E.R., Schwartz, J.H., Jessel, T.M. Principles of neural science. Appleton & Lance, Norwalk, Connecticut, 1991
35. La, B.N., Mandel, H.G., Way, E.L. Fundamentals of drug metabolism and drug disposition. Robert E. Krieger Publishing Company, Huntington, New York, 1979
36. Lampe, K.F., Fagerstrom, R. Plant toxicity and dermatitis: a manual for physicians. The Williams and Wilkinson Company, Baltimore, 1968
37. Lea, H. C. Materials toward a history of witchcraft. Thomas Yoseloff, New York, 1957
38. Leland, C.G. Aradia, or the gospel of the witches. David Nutt, London, 1899
39. le Strange, R. A history of herbal plants. Arco Publishing Company, Inc., New York, 1977
40. Levi-Strauss, C. The savage mind. The University of Chicago Press, Chicago, 1973
41. Lewis, W.H., Elvin-Lewis, M.P.F. Contributions of herbology to modern medicine and dentistry. In: Keeler, R.F., Tu, A.T. (Eds.) Handbook of natural toxins vol. 1, Plant and fungal toxins. Marcel Dekker, Inc. New York, pp 785-815, 1983
42. Loudon, J.C. Arboretum et Fruticetum Britanicum. Longman, Brown, Green, and Longmans, London, 1844
43. Lust, J.B. The herb book. Benedict Lust Publications, New York, 1974
44. Meyers, F.H., Jawetz, E., Goldfien, A. Review of medical parmacology. Lange Medical Publications, Los Altos, California, 1978

45. Monter, E.W. European witchcraft. John Woley & Sons, Inc., New York, 1969
46. Oakleaf, Z.D. Ozark mountain and European white witches. In:Watson, W.H. (Ed.) Black folk medicine. Transaction Books, New Brunswick, NJ, pp 71-86, 1984
47. Panter, K.E., Wierenga, T.L., Bunch, T.D. Ultrasonographic studies on the fetotoxic effects of poisonous plants in livestock. In: Keeler, R.F., Tu, A.T. (Eds.) Handbook of natural toxins vol. 6, Toxicology of plant and fungal compounds. Marcel Dekker, Inc. New York, pp 589-606, 1983
48. Pitt-Rivers, J. Spiritual power in Central America: The naguals of Chiapas. In: Douglas, M. (ed.) Witchcraft confessions and accusations. Tavistock publications, London, pp 183-206, 1970
49. Pocs, E. Fairies and witches at the boundary of South-Eastern and Central Europe. FF Communications No. 243. Academia Scientarum Fennika, Helsinki, 1989
50. Ponhola, J., Harpf, M. Determinantion of atropine and obidoxime in automatic injection devices used as antidotes against nerve agent intoxication. Journal of Chromatography 686:350-354, 1994
51. Robinson, G.D. Absorption from the vagina. The Journal of Pharmacy and Experimental Therapy 32: 81-88, 1927
52. Russell, J.B. Witchcraft in the Middle Ages. Cornell University Press, London, 1972
53. Schenk, G. The book of poisons. Rinehart & Company, Inc., New York, 1955
54. Schultes, R.E., Hofmann, A. Plants of the Gods. McGraw-Hill Company, New York, 1979
55. Scot, R. The discoverie of witchcraft. Southern Illinois University Press, Illinois, 1964
56. Shulgin, A.T. Chemistry of psychotomimetics. In: Hoffmeister, F. and Stille, G. (Eds.) Psychotropic agents. Part III., pp 3-29, Springer-Verlag Berlin, 1982
57. Simons, G.L. The witchcraft world. Barnes and Noble Books, New York, 1974
58. Summers, M. The history of witchcraft and demonology. The Citadel Press, Secaucus, NJ, 1971

59. Tavenner, E. Canidia and other witches. In: Levack, B.P. Witchcraft in the ancient world and the middle ages. Garland Publishing Inc., New York & London, pp. 14-39, 1992
60. Thomas, W. Proceedings against Dame Alice Kyteler. Camden Society, 1843 (cited by Summers 1971)
61. Topalov, V., Gavrilov M., Jankulov, J. Herbs and herb harvesting (in Bulgarian). Hristo G. Danov, Plovdiv, 1983
62. Weyer, J. Witches, devils, and doctors in the Renaissance (De praestigiis daemonum). Medieval & Renaissance Texts & Studies, Binghamton, NY, 1991
63. Ziboorg, G. The medical man and the witch during the Renaissance. The Johns Hopkins Press, Baltimore, 1935

Notes on other literature sources

INDEX

Aconitum , 41-44
   napellus
   ferox
   lycotonum
   vulparia
Aconite, 42-45
Acorum (see also Acorus calamus), 41, 72
Acorus calamus, 71
Alkaloids, 26-28
    Definition, 26
    Groups, 26
    Tropane, 28
Albertini, Alnardo, 5
Amphibians, 34, 36
Anadenanthera, 34
Antidote, 85
Andagoya, Pascual de, 4
Apium petroselinum, 66
Ascorbic acid, 72
Apulieus, 73
Atropa belladonna, 45, 84
Atropine, 26, 28, 46-47, 52, 57, 61, 84-85, 87-90
Balkan Penisnsula, 14, 73
Beladonna, 46-47,
Benandanti, 91
Bouquet, Henry, 5
Bufo alvarius, 34
Bufonidae, 34
Bufotalidin, 35
Bulgaria(n), 14-15, 94
Caffeine, 27
Cardano, Girolamo, 20, 70
Carum petroselinum, 66

Caul, 92
Christmas rose, 34
Cicuta, 47, 49
Cicuta virosa, 47-49
Cicutoxin, 47
Clavicep purpurea, 31
Commiphora, 59
Colchicum autumnale, 32
Coniine, 27, 48, 50,
Conium maculatum, 48-49, 76
Cornus sanguinea, 95
Culpeper, Nicholas, 41, 50, 54, 61, 62, 68, 70, 71
Daphne laureola, 73
Darnel, 53
Datura, 55-59
    arborea
    ceratocaula
    floripondio
    inoxia
    stramonium
De ecclesiasticis disciplinis, 5
Deadly Nightshade, 28, 45, 47, 62, 63, 84
De prestigiis daemonum, 18
Delrio, Martin, 4
Demon(s), 3, 13-14, 61
Dendrites, 85
Devil, 3-9, 13, 53, 66-67, 81, 94
Digitalis purpurea, 34, 60
Dioscorides, 21, 44, 51
Discourse Des Sorceress, 5
Electroencephalogram, 87
Epipedobates tricolor, 35
Ergot, 37
Euphorbia lathyris, 68

Folliculitis, 84
Formicarius, 4
Foxglove, 61, 75
Gemini, 63
Hellebrigenin, 35
Helleborus niger, 34
Henbane, black, 28, 51-53, 57, 84
Hemlock, 47-50, 60
    spotted, 48-49
    water, 48
Hortus Sanitatis, 63
Hyoscyamine, 21, 51-52, 57
Hyoscyamus niger, 51
Jimsonweed, 28, 55-56
Karakondzhuli, 15
Krosnojhazlitsa, 94
Kyteler, Lady Alice, 3, 9
Laguna, 8-9, 21
Lamia, 19
Laurel, 73
    dwarf
    spurge
Leprosy, 53
Libbard's-bane, 42
Lolium temulentum, 53
Lophophora williamsii, 59
Lupinus, 29
    albus
    angustifolius
    caudatus
    formosus
    sericeus
    luteus
Lycanthropy, 13
Macbeth, 33

Macht, David, 90
Mandragora officinarum, 64, 65
Mandrake root, 21, 63
Marmaritis, 69
Mattioli, Pier Andrea, 44
Monkshood, 42, 45
Mescaline, 89
Myrrh, 24, 60
Myrtle, 71
Newts, 35-36
Nicotine, 26
Nider, Johannes, 4
Night shade, 46, 62
Nymphea alba, 71
Ointment
    Definition, 3
    experimentation, 75-77
    preparation, 75
Olisbos, 94
Opium, 26-27
Paeonia, 69-70
    corralina
    lactiflora
    officinalis
    suffruticosa
    veitchii
Papaver somniferum, 27
Papaverine, 27
Peony (see Paeonia)
Penis coriaceus, 94
Peyote, 59
Pitt Rivers Museum, 12
Plato, 49
Pliny, 42

Index

Podophyllum pelatum, 63
Populus spp., 54
Porta, Giovanni Batista, 20, 65
Psychotomimetics, 87
Ranunculaceae, 69
Regino, Abbot, 5
Romeo and Juliet, 44
Rumex, 62
    acetosa
    acetosella
Sabbat, 3-5
Salamanders, 36
Salazar, Alonsode, 8, 82
Samandarin. 36
Samodiva(s), 92
Sesquiterpenes, 60
Socrates, 49
Solanaceae, 45, 51, 55
Solanum dulcamara, 63
Sorghum, 95
Sorrel, 62
Spurge, 68-69, 73
Sweet Flag, 71
Sweet sedge (see Sweet Flag)
Synapse, 85-87
Teratology, 31
Tiger, 37-38
Thornapple, 55
Toads, 33-34
Tritutrus, 36
    alpestris
    cristatus
    marmoratus
    vulgaris
Umbelliferae, 47-48, 66

Vagina, 89-90
Vervain, 61-62
Virgo, 63
Water Lily, 21, 71
Werewolf demons, 14-15
Weyer, Johann, 18-20, 24
Wolfsbane, 43

About the author

Alexander Kuklin earned his Ph.D. in the Program of Plant Physiology and Genetics at the University of Tennessee in Knoxville, Tennessee and has published extensively in peer reviewed scientific journals on physiological processes of plants and plant tissue cultures. He conducted his postdoctoral studies at the Oak Ridge National Laboratory (Oak Ridge, TN). This book is a result of his academic training combined with herbalist experience and practices. Dr. Kuklin has also interests in the relationship between science and the occult. He is presently working for a biotechnology company in California.

If you would like to share your comments on the book or your experiences, e-mail them to kuklina@hotmail.com.

Address correspondence via the publisher.

✍ Notes on the Flying Ointment